Collins · *do brilliantly !*

RevisionGuide

KS3 English

Pam Bloomfield

Series Editor: Jayne de Courcy

CONTENTS AND REVISION PLANNER

The Test is for Year 9 students and takes place in May. You will be given the actual dates by your teacher.

There are three papers in the English Test, each giving you an opportunity to show your different skills.

Reading Paper: 1 hour, plus 15 minutes' reading time

You are given three extracts to read and study, two non-fiction texts and one fiction text. There are then about 14 questions, some short, some longer, on different aspects of the texts. The questions focus particularly on the way they have been written and the effects they create on the reader.

Writing Paper: 1 hour 30 minutes

In this paper you will have two writing tasks to complete.

Section A

Contains the longer writing task, which tests your skills on an extended piece of writing. You should spend:

- 15 minutes planning your response on the planning page opposite the task. (This is not marked.)
- 45 minutes writing and checking your response.

Section B

Contains the shorter writing task, which tests your skills on a sharply focused writing task where you need to write with precision. You should spend:

- 5 minutes planning (as there is no planning page, you will need to create your own).
- 25 minutes writing and checking your response.

Shakespeare: 45 minutes

There will be **one** question on the Shakespeare play that you have studied. There will also be extracts from the scenes you have studied to refer to in your response.

Levels of achievement

By the end of Key Stage 3, most students are between levels 3 and 7. A typical 14-year-old will achieve a level 5 or 6 in their National Test.

What about Speaking and Listening?

Speaking and listening will be assessed by your English teacher as part of your normal work in class. It will become part of your 'Teacher Assessment' levels that your teacher gives for your achievements in English through the work you have completed during the year.

TEST TIPS

On these two pages, you can find the key comments from the most recent KS3 English National Test.

Reading Paper

As a first step, students should always remember to go back to the text when looking for the answer to a question.

Short quotations that 'pin point' evidence are far more effective than longer ones where the examiner has to 'guess' which part is relevant.

Generally there should be a greater awareness of the way in which the structure of a text – the way its beginning is linked to the ending – contributes to its effectiveness.

Students should be able to recognise, and write about, how writers create effects such as tension and suspense.

The ability to understand and explain how words are used, plus the impact they have on the reader, is central to success on the Reading Paper.

Students often know what a word means, but they need to be more aware of implied meanings within the context of the text itself.

It is not enough simply to identify figurative language; students must be able to explain the meaning and effect it creates.

Answers that rely on re-telling the story fail to recognise the significance of the question. Few, if any, responses require this approach; students should analyse questions more carefully before they respond.

Confident students are able to use well-chosen, precise quotations embedded into their comments, to explain the impact on the reader.

It is disappointing to see how many students lose marks by not even attempting to answer some of the questions on the Reading Paper.

Writing Paper

Students need to be able to maintain a consistent purpose and viewpoint in their writing if they are to achieve at least a level 5.

Neglecting punctuation is a common error that prevents some students from achieving their potential in writing.

Good writers can draw on a number of stylistic techniques such as repetition, rhetorical questions and alliteration, to emphasise their points and create effects.

Paragraphs must be used to structure texts, reflecting the content - rather than an arbitrary break every 10 or 15 lines or so.

More attention needs to be paid to making effective links between sentences. These should signal different stages of what is being said and how one point relates to another, rather than simply making point after point. This will help to order and develop the content.

Most students were able to adapt their writing to the task given, engaging the attention of the readers, but too many were only able to use very basic stylistic features with limited vocabulary.

At higher levels students need to be able to use a wider range of punctuation to make their writing clear, develop ideas and guide the reader.

To achieve the highest marks for spelling, students not only need to be accurate, they must also use a wide ranging vocabulary that tests and demonstrates their skill.

Using varied sentence structures, with accurate internal punctuation, is the sign of a skilled writer - who creates interest for the reader.

HOW THIS BOOK WILL HELP YOU...

This book will help you to revise what you have learnt in your English lessons and to prepare you for your KS3 English Test.

What this book contains

The first three sections of the book revise important skills and help you focus on the types of questions and tasks you will meet in each of your Test papers. The next two sections contain Test Practice, sample answers and marking guidance. Each section is described below.

FOCUS ON READING This section helps you tackle different types of questions on a variety of different texts. These questions are of the kind you will meet in your Reading Paper. You are shown how to answer questions and how marks are awarded.

FOCUS ON WRITING This section revises the different aspects of writing that you need in order to do well in your Writing Paper.

FOCUS ON SHAKESPEARE This section explains the different types of questions you could be given on your set play.

TEST PRACTICE This section contains sample Reading and Writing Test Papers for you to try, followed by answers and guidance. The marking schemes provided are totally in line with those that will be used by the examiners of your English Test.

HOW WELL HAVE YOU DONE? In this final section you'll find sample answers to the questions and tasks given in the first three sections of the book, with guidance on how to tackle them.

How to use this book effectively

Everyone has different concerns and weak spots. The way in which you tackle the contents of this book will therefore largely be up to you. It has been divided up into a number of short revision sessions so that it is flexible and easy to use at home.

As a general guide, there are two approaches that will probably work best. Option 1 and Option 2 are described next.

OPTION 1 TOTAL REVISION!

This option is the one we would recommend for everyone who has the time and the determination to really want to do as well as they can in their KS3 English National Test.

Start at the beginning with Focus on Reading and work your way through to the end of the book. To do this properly, you will need to:

- start as early as you can – in January ideally;
- think carefully about how much time you will need for each section;
- work out a careful revision schedule – the division of the book into short revision sessions will help with this (see the contents and revision planner);
- pace yourself and try not to feel under too much pressure;
- give yourself a little extra time at the end to revisit sections just before the Test.

OPTION 2 SELECTED HIGHLIGHTS

If you are short of time, you may feel that you want to select certain revision sessions where you feel you particularly need help:

- examine the different revision sessions carefully and what they have to offer;
- choose the areas where you feel you need the most help (not the ones that look interesting or easy!);
- give yourself a little extra time at the end to revisit sections just before the Test.

SUGGESTIONS FOR WAYS OF WORKING

✓ Set aside some space so you can work without distractions.

✓ Tell other people in the house what you are doing and why it is important that you aren't disturbed.

✓ Switch off your mobile, TV, computer and anything else that may distract you.

✓ Have everything that you are going to need, such as pens, paper etc., ready to use.

✓ Refer to your revision plan to guide your work.

✓ Take a break every half hour, get up and move around for a minute or two.

✓ Know when you are going to stop and keep to it.

✓ If you don't complete all that you aimed to do in the allotted time, set another time when you can continue. Don't just go on and on into the night.

✓ **Give yourself a reward for keeping to your schedule!**

A Word of Advice

Whichever option you choose, you should also:

- Avoid dipping and diving through the contents in a haphazard way or you may find yourself becoming very confused as a result.

- Follow the instructions carefully and complete the work that is suggested. Don't just say to yourself, 'Oh yes, I can do that!' and charge on to the next bit. DO IT. Write down your answers and check them against the ones given at the back of the book. If you find some of the tasks easy, getting them right will help to boost your confidence.

- Don't look at the answers and guidance at the back of the book until you are ready. If something is difficult, have a go anyway, and when you really can't do any more, THEN go to the back for help.

Retrieving information from a text

In your English Test Reading Paper you will be expected to be able to:

'Describe, select or retrieve information, events or ideas from texts.'

Read the following extract:

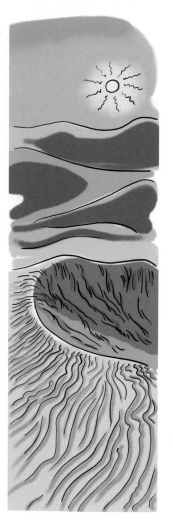

The Takla Makan Desert

May 1st 1894
The night was cold; the thermometer fell to 35 degrees Fahr.
(2 degrees C), the lowest reading we had during the twenty-six days
we were crossing the desert. But the atmosphere was pure, and the
stars glittered with incomparable brilliancy. The morning dawned
calm and gloriously bright – not a speck of cloud in the sky, not a
breath of wind on the tops of the dunes. No sooner had the sun risen
than it began to be warm … All the previous day I had not tasted a
drop of water. But suffering the extreme torture of thirst, I ventured
to swallow about a tumblerful of the horrible and abominable
concoction which the Chinese call brandy, stuff that we carried
to burn in our Primus cooking-stove. It burned my throat like oil
of vitriol …

May 7th 1894
I now changed my course to due south-east. Why so? Why did I not
keep on towards the east, as I had always done hitherto? I do not
know. Perhaps the moon bewitched me; for she showed her silver
crescent in that quarter of the heavens and shed down a dim, pale
blue illumination over the silent scene. Leaning on the spade-shaft,
I plodded away at a steady pace in a straight line towards the south-
east, as though I were being led by an unseen, but irresistible hand. At
intervals I was seized by a traitorous desire to sleep, and was obliged to
stop and rest. My pulse was excessively weak; I could scarcely discern
its beats. I had to steel myself by the strongest effort of will to prevent
myself dropping off to sleep. I was afraid that if I did go off, I should
never awaken again. I walked with my eyes riveted upon the moon.
And kept expecting to see its silver belt glittering on the dark waters
of the stream. But no such sight met my eyes. The whole of the east
quarter was enshrouded in the cool night mist.

From *My Life as an Explorer* by Sven Hedin

[handwritten margin note: ? fahrenite meaning unit of measurement in measurement temperature Britain]

> **1 Create a 'Fact File' giving information about the Takla Makan Desert.** *(2 marks)*

Begin by highlighting the information (the facts) that are given in the diary entry for May 1st 1894. One point has been done for you. Then select the details you have highlighted to help you to complete the chart below:

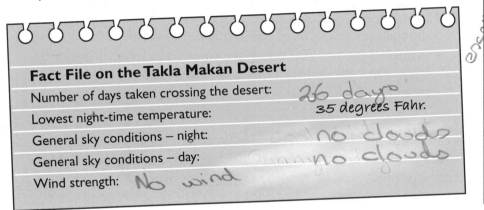

Fact File on the Takla Makan Desert

Number of days taken crossing the desert: *26 days*

Lowest night-time temperature: *35 degrees Fahr.*

General sky conditions – night: *no clouds*

General sky conditions – day: *no clouds*

Wind strength: *No wind*

'DESCRIBE EVENTS, CHARACTERS OR IDEAS FROM A TEXT'

> **2 Describe Hedin's journey on May 7th in no more than 40 words.** *(5 marks)*

The second entry in Hedin's diary describes part of his journey across the desert, but the facts are mixed in with personal comments about his experience. To answer the question successfully, you must focus only on the facts. You need to:
- begin by highlighting the facts of the journey itself (omit the extra details of Hedin's commentary);
- make a draft list of the facts on a piece of paper and count the words – aim for about 20–25 words;
- cross out less important details if you have too many words;
- write your response in the space below by putting your listed events into proper sentences, using your own words in order to give a summary of the events.

_____

_____

_____

_____

_____

Answers and guidance are on pages 104–105.

esc plaining the meaning

Interpreting information from a text

In your English Reading Paper, marks are awarded for how well you can:

'Deduce, infer or interpret information, events or ideas from texts.'

- **Deduce** means that you need to 'read beneath the surface of the text' to discover more than the author states.
- **Infer** means that you have to use your reasoning powers to draw conclusions from the information given.
- **Interpret** means that you have to explain what is going on from what the author writes, e.g. why someone behaves as he or she does.

read with cosont rg t o a

Read the following extract and as you do so ask yourself: 'How much more information can I gain through deduction, inference and interpretation, by reading beyond the words?'

Using a highlighter, annotate the points where you think more can be drawn out of the text. Some have already been done to start you off:

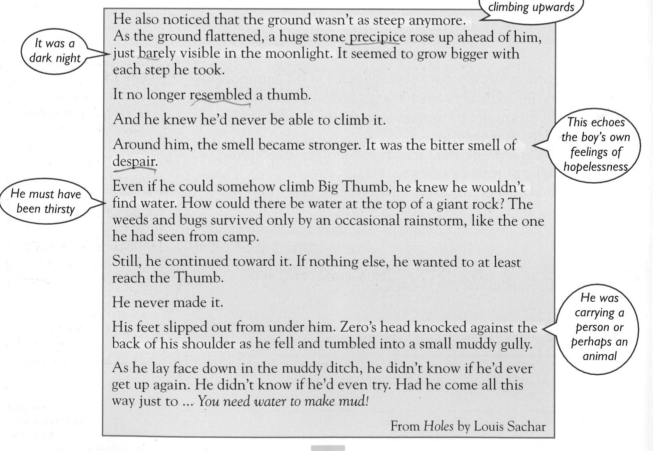

He had been climbing upwards

He also noticed that the ground wasn't as steep anymore. As the ground flattened, a huge stone _precipice_ rose up ahead of him, just barely visible in the moonlight. It seemed to grow bigger with each step he took.

It was a dark night

It no longer resembled a thumb.

And he knew he'd never be able to climb it.

Around him, the smell became stronger. It was the bitter smell of despair.

This echoes the boy's own feelings of hopelessness

Even if he could somehow climb Big Thumb, he knew he wouldn't find water. How could there be water at the top of a giant rock? The weeds and bugs survived only by an occasional rainstorm, like the one he had seen from camp.

He must have been thirsty

Still, he continued toward it. If nothing else, he wanted to at least reach the Thumb.

He never made it.

His feet slipped out from under him. Zero's head knocked against the back of his shoulder as he fell and tumbled into a small muddy gully.

He was carrying a person or perhaps an animal

As he lay face down in the muddy ditch, he didn't know if he'd ever get up again. He didn't know if he'd even try. Had he come all this way just to ... *You need water to make mud!*

From *Holes* by Louis Sachar

> **1 From the extract what do you learn about the conditions and setting in which the boy was making his journey? Give two examples from the text and explain what each tells us.**
>
> *(4 marks)*

Here is one possible example:

Example: 'the ground wasn't steep anymore'
Explanation: This tells us that the boy had been climbing up a hill or a mountain.

> *I mark will be awarded for the example (a quotation) and 1 for your explanation.*

Now give two other examples of your own:

Example: _____

Explanation: _____

Example: _____

Explanation: _____

> **2 Look at the section 'And he knew he'd never be able to climb it...' to '...he didn't know if he'd even try'. What do we learn about the boy's physical and emotional condition?** *(4 marks)*

Here is one possible answer about the boy's physical condition:

In this section we can tell that physically the boy is very tired. When he falls into the ditch it says, 'he didn't know if he'd ever get up again.'

Now find another point that could be made about his physical condition:

_____

_____

_____

What could you say about the boy's emotional condition?

_____

_____

_____

HINTS
- Supporting your answer with evidence from the text is essential. This means that you must give either a **close summary** of what has been said, or a **direct quotation**.
- Keep quotations brief (1–10 words) and remember to indicate that they are quotations by enclosing them in inverted commas: '...'

Answers and guidance are on page 105.

FOCUS ON READING

In your Test, early questions may ask you to deduce or infer fairly small details. You may then be given a question that expects you to use inference, deduction and interpretation in a less supported way.

Reread the extract on page 4 and then read this continuation of the story:

He crawled along the gully in the direction that seemed the muddiest. The ground became gloppier. The mud splashed up as he slapped the ground.

Using both hands, he dug a hole in the soggy soil. It was too dark to see, but he thought he could feel a tiny pool of water at the bottom of his hole. He stuck his head in the hole and licked the dirt.

He dug deeper, and as he did so, more water seemed to fill the hole. He couldn't see it, but he could feel it – first with his fingers, then with his tongue.

He dug until he had a hole that was about as deep as his arm was long. There was enough water for him to scoop out with his hands and drop on Zero's face.

Zero's eyes remained closed. But his tongue poked out between his lips, searching out the droplets.

Stanley dragged Zero closer to the hole. He dug, then scooped some more water and let it pour out of his hands into Zero's mouth.

As he continued to widen his hole, his hand came across a smooth, round object. It was too smooth and too round to be a rock.

He wiped the dirt off of it and realized it was an onion.

He bit into it without peeling it. The hot bitter juice burst into his mouth. He could feel it all the way up to his eyes. And when he swallowed, he felt its warmth move down his throat and into his stomach.

He only ate half. He gave the other half to Zero.
'Here, eat this.'
'What is it?' Zero whispered.
'A hot fudge sundae.'

From *Holes* by Louis Sachar, pages 171-2

3 Explain why, when Zero asks what he is being given to eat at the end of the extract, Stanley replies, '*A hot fudge sundae.*'

(4 marks)

_____

_____

_____

_____

_____

_____

_____

_____

_____

_____

_____

_____

_____

_____

_____

_____

_____

HINTS
- Answering a question like this requires you to 'read between the lines' and 'beyond the words'.
- Think about the context of the extract:
  - What do you know about the place that the boys have come to and their physical condition?
  - What has Stanley done so far to help Zero?
  - Is there a link between what Stanley is really giving Zero and what he says?
  - Is Stanley's response meant to be humorous or serious?

Answers and guidance are on page 106.

Commenting on the structure and organisation of a text

Several questions in your Test will expect you to analyse the structure of a text and comment on the way the writer has chosen to organise it – perhaps to create suspense or explain something clearly.

These sorts of questions also test your understanding of the way a writer uses different types of punctuation.

Silent Spring, by Rachel Carson, published in 1962, raised awareness of the chemical pollution of ground-water (the water that lies below the land's surface).

Read the following paragraph from the book and examine the way the author has organised the content into three distinct sections.

① ② ③

In the entire water-pollution problem, there is probably nothing more disturbing than the threat of widespread contamination of ground-water. It is not possible to add pesticides to water anywhere without threatening the purity of water everywhere. Seldom if ever does Nature operate in closed and separate compartments, and she has not done so in distributing the earth's water supply. Rain, falling on the land, settles down through pores and cracks in the soil and rock, penetrating deeper and deeper until eventually it reaches a zone where all the pores of the rock are filled with water, a dark, subsurface sea, rising under hills, sinking beneath valleys. This ground-water is always on the move, sometimes at a pace so slow that it travels no more than fifty feet a year, sometimes rapidly, by comparison, so that it moves nearly a tenth of a mile in a day. It travels by unseen waterways until here and there it comes to the surface as a spring, or perhaps it is tapped to feed a well. But mostly it contributes to streams and so to rivers. Except for what enters streams directly as rain or surface run-off, all the running water of the earth's surface was at one time ground-water. And so, in a very real and frightening sense, pollution of the ground-water is pollution of water everywhere.

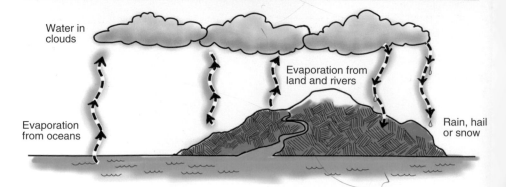

Water in clouds

Evaporation from land and rivers

Evaporation from oceans

Rain, hail or snow

> **1 How does the writer's structure and organisation within the paragraph help the reader to understand how ground-water pollution by pesticides is a threat to our water everywhere?**
>
> *(5 marks)*

You should:
- Describe the structure of the paragraph.
- Identify the development of ideas within the paragraph.
- **Comment on how well the writer has conveyed her ideas.**

Sample answer

Look at the colour coding of the response which shows how the student has addressed all parts of the question:

In the paragraph there are three sections, which help the reader to understand how water becomes polluted. The writer begins by making a statement, introducing the threat of ground-water pollution, from 'In the entire...' to '...the earth's water supply.' She is suggesting that pesticides used in one area will naturally move to another.

In order to explain how this can happen, she then describes the process that creates water underneath ground level, from 'Rain, falling...' to '...and so to rivers.' This demonstrates that water entering the ground at one level will reappear at another place later on in the cycle.

Finally, in the section beginning 'Except for...', she concludes that most of the earth's water comes from beneath the surface and therefore polluting ground-water is dangerous for water everywhere.

By giving the reader a clear first statement, and then following this with a detailed explanation of the process, we are led to a clear conclusion. This allows the reader to understand the water cycle and the danger of water pollution through pesticides.

HINTS
- Answer the question as a whole by responding to **all three bullet points.**
- **Structure your answer** to show that you have a good general understanding of how paragraphs work.
- Knit together all the points you make in a clear and interesting way, **using short quotes** if this helps to explain the points you make.

Apart from being asked to comment on the structure of a text, you may also be asked to explain why a writer has used various grammatical or presentational features and the effect they create.

The following is the continuation of the extract from Rachel Carson's book.

Read the extract and answer the questions on the opposite page.

Glossary

insecticides – *chemicals that destroy pests*
contaminated – *polluted*
transcends – *goes beyond*

It must have been by such a dark, underground sea that poisonous chemicals traveled from a manufacturing plant in Colorado to a farming district several miles away, there to poison wells, sicken humans and livestock, and damage crops – an extraordinary episode that may easily be only the first of many like it. Its history, in brief, is this. In 1943, the Rocky Mountain Arsenal of the Army Chemical Corps, located near Denver, began to manufacture war materials. Eight years later the facilities of the arsenal were leased to a private oil company for the production of insecticides. Even before the change of operations, however, mysterious reports had begun to come in. Farmers several miles from the plant began to report unexplained sickness among livestock; they complained of extensive crop damage. Foliage turned yellow, plants failed to mature, and many crops were killed outright. There were reports of human illness, thought by some to be related.

The irrigation waters on these farms were derived from shallow wells. When the well waters were examined … they were found to contain an assortment of chemicals … which had been discharged from the Rocky Mountain Arsenal into holding ponds during the years of its operation. Apparently the ground-water between the arsenal and the farms had become contaminated and it had taken seven to eight years for the wastes to travel underground a distance of about three miles from the holding ponds to the nearest farm. This seepage had continued to spread and had further contaminated an area of unknown extent. The investigators knew of no way to contain the contamination or halt its advance.

And so the story of the Colorado farms and their damaged crops assumes a significance that transcends its local importance. What other parallels may there be, not only in Colorado but wherever chemical pollution finds its way into public waters? In lakes and streams everywhere, in the presence of catalysing air and sunlight, what dangerous substances may be born of parent chemicals labelled 'harmless'?

Indeed, one of the most alarming aspects of the chemical pollution of water is the fact that here – in river or lake or reservoir, or for that matter in the glass of water served at your dinner-table – are mingled chemicals that no responsible chemist would think of combining in his laboratory. The possible interactions between these freely mixed chemicals are deeply disturbing… .

2 Explain the purpose and effect of the following punctuation marks used by the writer:

(a) The dash in line 4 *'and damage crops – an extraordinary episode'*.

(b) The inverted commas around the word 'harmless' in the last line of the third paragraph. *(2 marks)*

_____

_____

_____

_____

3 Comment on the effect and purpose of the questions used in the extract below:

What other parallels may there be, not only in Colorado but wherever chemical pollution finds its way into public waters? In lakes and streams everywhere, in the presence of catalysing air and sunlight, *what dangerous substances may be born of parent chemicals labelled 'harmless'?*

(2 marks)

_____

_____

_____

_____

4 Explain how the writer uses the opening sentence of each paragraph as signals to the reader. *(4 marks)*

_____

_____

_____

_____

_____

_____

HINTS

- Questions about how a writer uses punctuation and grammar expect you to show that a writer uses these to communicate something extra to the reader. As well as being able to point out what the writer has done, you also need to write about the effect that has been created.
- Brackets and dashes are often used to add an extra piece of information as an aside to the reader.
- Inverted commas can mean a quotation or that the writer is using a word or phrase in a particular way.
- Writers may use questions to make readers think of answers themselves – they can be almost like a challenge to the reader.
- Words and phrases at the beginning of paragraphs can act as signals to the reader to indicate, for example, the development of an argument, e.g. 'on the other hand', 'however', or an order, e.g. 'Firstly', 'Finally'.

Answers and guidance are on pages 106–107.

FOCUS ON READING

Discussing a writer's style

> Commenting on a writer's style, including the tone and the use of individual words, is a very important focus for questions in the Reading Test.
>
> When writing about an author's style, you will need to use direct quotations from the text to pinpoint the exact words and phrases that illustrate your comments.

The following passage is a newspaper article on the champion cyclist Nicole Cooke. The annotations at the side point out some of the features of style.

Cooke ready to take on the world

Time-trial and mountain-bike champion hits the road

William Fotheringham in Lisbon

No Briton has ever started a world road race championship as the overwhelming favourite, but that is the status Nicole Cooke will enjoy in Monsanto Park this morning when she defends the women's junior title she won last year in Brittany.

'Enjoy' is perhaps not the most appropriate word: Cooke will be a heavily marked woman. The rest of the 64-rider field know full well that her back wheel is the best one to follow, and that if they can stay in her slipstream to the finish they may stand a chance of winning the gold medal.

Surprise is a key weapon in a road race but it is no longer part of Cooke's armoury. Since she sprinted across the line in Plouay in October with a yell of delight to become Britain's first ever junior road race champion, male or female, she has added the mountain-bike title and, on Tuesday, the time-trial gold.

She has no team-mates to help her, so her main ally today is the course, with its two hills. 'I'm definitely going to be marked, but this course is hard enough for the race to split up; hopefully it will, and a small group will be easier to deal with. Last year I won from a break, but the bunch could have pulled us back perhaps, but this course is so hard that a selection will be made of the best riders.'

Her triple of medals across the three disciplines in the space of 12 months is already unprecedented, and today she is chasing another record: no junior man or woman has successfully defended a world road race title, simply because the titles usually go to a second-year junior and the following year he or she will be racing at senior level.

In the seven years since she began cycling, however, Cooke has acquired a taste for records, according to her mentor, the former professional Shane Sutton, who is the Welsh national cycling coach. Sutton was renowned for his hardness, but even he has been astounded at Cooke's competitive mentality. 'She likes to kill off the opposition; that's the way she's always been. It doesn't matter who it is, who she is up against, her tenacity is unbelievable.'

Annotations:

- Begins with a startling statement to gain the attention of the reader
- Introduces purpose – to inform readers of the race and the personality
- Technical term shows understanding of the subject
- Metaphoric imagery
- Personal detail uses informal language
- Quoting the 'star' adds weight to the article
- Superlative – a strong word to use in praise, indicates the writer's point of view
- Another quotation, this time from an expert

Born into a cycling family, coached by her father Tony, Cooke has dispensation to race against the men and is no shrinking violet: last year, Julian Winn, a seasoned British international, watched in astonishment as she attacked for an early lap prize. 'He couldn't believe what was going on,' chuckles Sutton. 'I told him it was just Nicole putting the boot in.' If Sutton admires Cooke's coolness under the pressure of a big occasion, he is astonished by her versatility.

An articulate 18-year-old who has just passed A-levels in maths, geography and biology, Cooke would have been selected for Sydney last year had she not fallen foul of a rule that keeps junior cyclists out of the Games. An Olympic gold is her big aim within cycling, but this is not a goal acquired recently: interviewed at the age of 12, she said that gold in Athens was her goal.

Whatever the outcome today, Cooke now has to choose a course for the next few years. Sutton is a down-to-earth Australian, not given to hyperbole, but he is effusive. 'I'm sure if she goes into the right system she can be Olympic champion in Athens. She obviously has the ability, but she needs the right pathway from here on in.' In fact he goes further, far further: 'She can be the best women's road racer of all time.'

Humorous, more light-hearted tone

Informal expression gives a 'human' feeling

Contrasting formal tone introduces a more serious subject

Signals the conclusion to the article

Glossary
hyperbole – *exaggeration, overstatement*

Rounded, positive note to end on

Look at the questions below and the sample answers that a student has given.

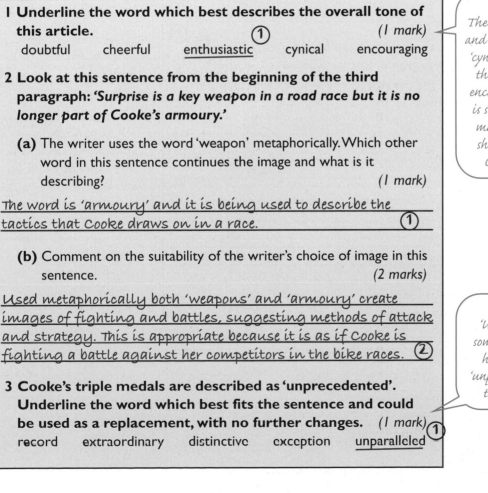

1 Underline the word which best describes the overall tone of this article. (1 mark) ①

doubtful   cheerful   <u>enthusiastic</u>   cynical   encouraging

2 Look at this sentence from the beginning of the third paragraph: *'Surprise is a key weapon in a road race but it is no longer part of Cooke's armoury.'*

(a) The writer uses the word 'weapon' metaphorically. Which other word in this sentence continues the image and what is it describing? (1 mark)

<u>The word is 'armoury' and it is being used to describe the tactics that Cooke draws on in a race.</u> ①

(b) Comment on the suitability of the writer's choice of image in this sentence. (2 marks)

<u>Used metaphorically both 'weapons' and 'armoury' create images of fighting and battles, suggesting methods of attack and strategy. This is appropriate because it is as if Cooke is fighting a battle against her competitors in the bike races.</u> ②

3 Cooke's triple medals are described as 'unprecedented'. Underline the word which best fits the sentence and could be used as a replacement, with no further changes. (1 mark) ①

record   extraordinary   distinctive   exception   <u>unparalleled</u>

COMMENT:
The writing is very positive and therefore 'doubtful' and 'cynical' are out. Although the tone is cheerful and encouraging, 'enthusiastic' is stronger and is a better match for the optimism shown in the article for Cooke's achievement.

COMMENT:
'Unprecedented' means something that has never happened before. Only 'unparalleled' also suggests this special meaning.

4 Focus on the last part of the article, from _'In the seven years...'_ to the end.

(a) The writer uses idiomatic and colloquial expressions such as 'putting the boot in'. Find two other examples from this section and explain what they mean. *(2 marks)*

The writer uses the phrase 'no shrinking violet' to describe Nicole, suggesting she is not afraid of attention. Later, Sutton is described as 'down-to-earth' implying that he is level-headed and practical. ②

(b) Why do you think the writer has chosen to use these familiar expressions? *(1 mark)*

In this section the writer is telling us more about Nicole's life and personality and therefore the style needs to be more informal. The familiar expressions he uses are more relaxed in tone and more in keeping with the human side of the content. ①

(c) Do you think these expressions are appropriate? *(1 mark)*

I think these expressions are appropriate because they sound more natural and help the reader to identify with people more easily than they would if more formal language was used. ①

5 In the final paragraph, the writer says that Sutton, Cooke's coach, is _'not given to hyperbole, but he is effusive'_.

(a) Find two examples in the passage where effusive, flattering adjectives have been used. *(2 marks)*

overwhelming   unbelievable ②

(b) Explain how the use of these adjectives matches the tone of the article in general. *(2 marks)*

The article gives a very upbeat, positive image of Nicole Cooke and her success as a cycling champion, saying things like 'her back wheel is the best one to follow' and talks about her 'chasing another record'. The adjectives contribute to this enthusiastic tone, for example, 'overwhelming' and 'unbelievable' create the impression that Cooke is the very best, incredible and an inspiration to others. ②

> **COMMENT:**
> _This question indirectly asks you to say what you think the tone of the passage in general is. It is a good idea to make this clear at the start of your answer. The comment about the adjectives then fits and follows naturally._

HINTS

- Questions on language assume that you understand terms such as **verb**, **adjectives** etc., so make sure you know them.
- It is also expected that you are familiar with terms describing figurative language such as **metaphors** and **similes**.
- Watch out for questions that are not as straightforward as they seem. You may need to do some thinking to understand the full response that is required to gain full marks.

Now it's your turn to answer questions on an author's style.
Read the passage below and answer the questions that follow.

Break for the Borders

Britain's newest mountain-bike trail opened in Glentress Forest last week

Alf Alderson tests his mettle with the pedals

Weather, Scotland and mountain biking are not three words that go readily together – **it takes a special kind of dedication and a great deal of fleece and Goretex to venture out into the mud and rain of the Scottish hills on your bike.**

Unless, that is, you head to a spot like Glentress Forest in the Borders, where the Forestry Commission has constructed some superb trails that allow for year-round riding. The freely drained tracks remain rideable in the worst rain, snow and sleet that Scotland can throw at you. Indeed, the fact that **they snake beneath thick forest canopies** for the most part also means that there's some shelter from the elements, particularly the biker's worst enemy – the wind.

Situated two miles east of Peebles, Glentress is now the number-one outdoor attraction in the Borders region, with more than 130,000 visitors last year who came here to hike, bike, ride a horse (there are trails for all three) or just to enjoy a picnic at one of the forest's fine viewpoints. And five miles east, **Red Bull has recently completed a new downhill course for mountain bikers who require such things as 14ft drop-offs to have a good day in the country.**

To date more than £100,000 has been spent on the mountain-bike trails at Glentress, most of it from Lottery funding. The Forestry Commission's regional recreation manager Jeremy Thompson says that more money is being sought from the Lottery to develop further trails.

The decision to focus on mountain biking at Glentress came about, Thompson says, after the marked increase in bikers using the forest over the past 10 years. 'A lot of them were getting bored with the forest roads and were heading off on to forest walks, where there was a danger of collisions with walkers – so we decided to put in some purpose-built trails.'

So what are the new trails like? Well, because Glentress Forest is the oldest Forestry Commission woodland in southern Scotland, with planting stretching as far back as 1920, there's a reasonable amount of trees for a start. That said, there are still a few ruler-edge boundaries – in fact the superb Black Trail follows one of these as you start your descent after the long climb to Dunslair Heights at 600m, but that's easily forgotten when you take in the sweeping views across the wild, open moorland above the Tweed Valley.

All the routes are built so that, whatever your ability, the ascents are rarely too steep or technical to ride. But it's the descents that you really go for, and these are a fine commendation to the trailbuilders' skills, taking in everything from twisty, cambered single-track to tricky stream crossings on wobbly planks, **intimidatingly steep descents**, sections over rocks and tree roots, and a nice blast down wide-open fire roads to finish at the car park (where there's a hose to clean your bike and maybe yourself).

Interestingly, the routes are also designed with conservation in mind – one of the requirements of the Forestry Commission was that not only should they be rideable in all weather, they should also have a working life of 20–25 years. The whole lot is charted on trail maps available at the car park, although you scarcely need these as the markings on the ground are so good.

I have to say that if Glentress and other Forestry Commission sites are the way mountain biking is set to go in Britain, there won't be any reason to travel abroad soon, because we really do have some world-class trails in these centres – and the views aren't bad either. But how about a ski lift to the top?

---

1 The article begins by making a comment about cycling in Scotland: 'it takes a special kind of dedication and a great deal of fleece and Goretex to venture out into the mud and rain of the Scottish hills on your bike.'
   (a) Which of the following do you think best sums up what the writer is saying? (underline your choice)   (1 mark)
      • You have to dress up in warm wool if you want to cycle in Scotland.
      • Only well-wrapped-up lunatics willingly brave the wet Scottish weather on a bike.
      • Cycling in Scotland is only for those who are devoted to the sport.
      • Cycling fanatics will confront the wet and sludge of Scotland only if they are warmly dressed.
   (b) Find another quotation that makes a negative comment about Scotland's weather in a similar tone.   (1 mark)

   _____

2 'they snake beneath thick forest canopies' (paragraph 2)
   Comment on the imagery the author has chosen to use here.   (2 marks)

   _____

   _____

3 'Red Bull has recently completed a new downhill course for mountain bikers who require such things as 14ft drop-offs to have a good day in the country.' (end of the third paragraph)
   (a) Explain the writer's sense of humour in this sentence.   (2 marks)

   _____

   _____

   _____

   _____

   (b) Find another example of the writer's humour.   (1 mark)

   _____

Answers and guidance are on pages 108–109.

4 'intimidatingly steep descents' *(in the seventh paragraph)*
The writer has invented an adverb, 'intimidatingly', from the adjective 'intimidating'. Underline the word from the following list that you think would make the best replacement. *(1 mark)*

scary   frighteningly   menacing   threateningly   terrifyingly

5 Examine the paragraph that begins 'So what are the new trails like?' How does the author persuade the reader that these trails would be worth visiting?

(4 marks)

_____

_____

_____

_____

_____

_____

6 Explain why you think 'Break for the Borders' is a suitable and effective title for this article. *(2 marks)*

_____

_____

_____

_____

HINTS

- Develop an awareness of the **style and tone** of a passage as you are reading it through before starting to write.
- Underline or highlight points of interest concerning **humour, informal/slang expressions**, **imagery** and **vocabulary** on your second reading of the extracts.
- Use a variety of **examples and quotations** in your answers, even if one that you have previously given fits the next question as well.
- **Answer all parts of the question**, even if it seems difficult – you may pick up a mark, but if you write nothing, you won't!

Answers and guidance are on pages 109–110.

FOCUS ON READING

In your Reading Test, being able to comment on the effect a text has on the reader, as well as appreciating the writer's purpose and viewpoint, is an essential skill.

Questions of this sort probably carry more marks than any of the other skills tested in the Reading Paper.

It may well be that you are given a poem as one of the three texts you have to study in the Reading Test.

Read the poem below, 'Dead Water', by the Chinese poet Wen Yi-Tuo, and examine what effects he creates, how he creates them and why. Some annotations have been made at the side to show you how you can engage with the text. Add some more of your own.

HINT
- Make sure you understand the terms **imagery**, **figurative language** and **personification**. If you need reminding, use the glossary at the back of the book.

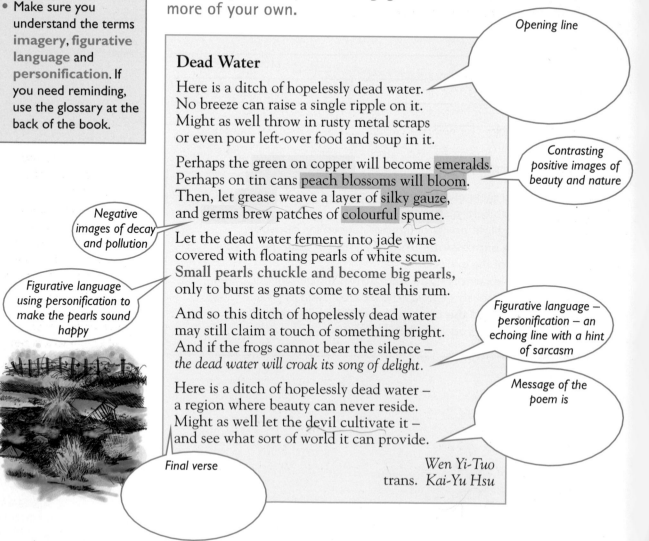

Opening line

Contrasting positive images of beauty and nature

Negative images of decay and pollution

Figurative language using personification to make the pearls sound happy

Figurative language – personification – an echoing line with a hint of sarcasm

Message of the poem is

Final verse

Dead Water

Here is a ditch of hopelessly dead water.
No breeze can raise a single ripple on it.
Might as well throw in rusty metal scraps
or even pour left-over food and soup in it.

Perhaps the green on copper will become emeralds.
Perhaps on tin cans peach blossoms will bloom.
Then, let grease weave a layer of silky gauze,
and germs brew patches of colourful spume.

Let the dead water ferment into jade wine
covered with floating pearls of white scum.
Small pearls chuckle and become big pearls,
only to burst as gnats come to steal this rum.

And so this ditch of hopelessly dead water
may still claim a touch of something bright.
And if the frogs cannot bear the silence –
the dead water will croak its song of delight.

Here is a ditch of hopelessly dead water –
a region where beauty can never reside.
Might as well let the devil cultivate it –
and see what sort of world it can provide.

Wen Yi-Tuo
trans. *Kai-Yu Hsu*

Look at the questions below and the sample answers that a student has given.

I **Discuss the effect the poet creates and the message he conveys through the contrasting images in the second stanza.**

(3 marks)

Sample answer

The poet has used images of polluted water such as 'green on copper', 'tin cans', 'grease', contrasting with objects of beauty ①
such as 'emeralds', 'peach blossoms' and 'silky gauze', in the second stanza. This contrast creates the effect of increasing the reader's disgust, for the pool of 'dead water' which people ①
have produced. Instead of seeing water as a source of life and a sign of cleanliness, through the poet's images we see it as diseased and dirty, a place where 'germs brew patches of ①
colourful spume'. It show us what the water should be like compared with what it has become.

---

2 **'Small pearls chuckle and become big pearls.'** *(3rd stanza)*
What effect is produced by this unusual line? *(2 marks)*

Sample answer

We know that pearls cannot chuckle and so this line immediately strikes the reader as odd. The poet's use of ①
personification suggests that there could be a sound of glee coming from the polluted water as it breeds the swarm of 'gnats' that are about to burst on the world, as if it is ①
taking its revenge.

---

3 **What do you think this poem is about? Discuss how the poet expresses his point of view through the poem and the effect this creates on you, the reader.** *(3 marks)*

Sample answer

This poem is about how people pollute the environment, they 'even pour left-over food and soup in it', showing that they ①
just don't care about what they are doing. The poet makes me feel awful because he is so sarcastic and offhand, as in ①
the lines
    'Let the dead water ferment into jade wine
        covered with floating pearls of white scum.'
where he is suggesting that no one cares and that includes me. By introducing brighter images such as 'peach ①
blossoms' and 'pearls' he reminds me that water should be beautiful too.

HINTS
The sample answer to question 3 is a good answer because the student has:
- Made a **point**, given **evidence** (using quotations) and then **commented** on it.
- Answered all parts of the question.
- Set out **quotations** correctly – note what happens when you need to quote two lines of a poem.
- Remembered to use 'I' because the question asks for the poem's effect 'on you', i.e., for a **personal opinion**.

Here is another poem, 'Frogless', by the Canadian writer Margaret Atwood, for you to study.

- Read it through carefully.
- Engage with the text and help yourself to understand the poem by annotating points that you think are interesting. For this purpose it is important to write on the page around the poem itself. Remember to do this in the Test too.
- Answer the questions on the opposite page.

Frogless

The sore trees cast their leaves
too early. Each twig pinching
shut like a jabbed clam.
Soon there will be a hot gauze of snow
searing the roots.

Booze in the spring runoff,
pure antifreeze;
the stream worms drunk and burning.
Tadpoles wrecked in the puddles.

Here comes an eel with a dead eye
grown from its cheek.
Would you cook it?
You would if.

The people eat sick fish
because there are no others.
Then they get born wrong.

This is not sport, sir.
This is not good weather.
This is not blue and green.

This is home.
Travel anywhere in a year, five years,
and you'll end up here.

Margaret Atwood

1 Discuss the effect created by the poet's image of the trees in the first stanza, including her use of figurative language.

(3 marks)

_____

_____

_____

_____

_____

_____

_____

2 (a) What effect does the verb 'wrecked' in the last line of the second stanza create?

(1 mark)

_____

_____

(b) *'You would if.'* What is the purpose of this last line of the third stanza?

(2 marks)

_____

_____

_____

_____

3 Explain how the last stanza helps you to understand why the poet has written this poem.

(4 marks)

_____

_____

_____

_____

_____

_____

_____

HINTS

- Read the poem once, then read the questions, then **read the poem again**.
- Engage with the poem by **highlighting or underlining points** or writing comments by the side after your second reading.
- 'Discuss the effect' means talk about **your reactions** to the poet's words and ideas, the effect they create on you.
- **The number of lines** given for you to write on help you to know how much you need to write.
- **The number of marks** should tell you how many points, pieces of evidence and comments you need to make.

Answers and guidance are on pages 110–111.

REVISION SESSION 1

Creating interesting sentences

> In the Writing Paper you will be assessed on several different aspects of the way you write.
>
> Sentences are an essential part of writing because they help to organise what you have to say. If you vary the structure of your sentences, as well as taking care with the punctuation, it will help you to achieve a high level.

WAYS TO ADD VARIETY TO YOUR SENTENCES

A sentence can be one word long, or several lines. As you write, think about the construction of your sentences and how they can be used to create interest. Here are some suggestions that will help you to add variety to your writing style.

1 START YOUR SENTENCES IN AN INTERESTING WAY

Many sentences begin in a straightforward way with a noun (or pronoun) at the beginning, followed by the verb.

For example: The boy ate his sandwich slowly.

This kind of sentence can be made more interesting simply by reorganising the order of the words.

For example, put the adverb first: *Slowly*, the boy ate his sandwich.

Starting a sentence like this, putting the emphasis on the adverb 'slowly', creates greater interest for the reader, because it sounds more intriguing.

A similar effect can be created by putting a verb at the beginning of a sentence.

For example: The gardener continued with his work and trimmed the hedge carefully could become: *Trimming the hedge carefully*, the gardener continued his work.

Now try this yourself with the sentences below:

(a) The librarian put the books back on the shelf fussily.

New version: _____

(b) The bird flew high into the sky and sang a song of joy.

New version: _____

Answers and guidance are on page 112.

2 USE A MIXTURE OF SIMPLE, COMPLEX AND COMPOUND SENTENCES

A **simple sentence** only has one clause:

> *Joe laughed cheerfully at the joke.*

A **complex sentence** has a main clause and one or more subordinate clauses, added to give extra information, which makes it more interesting. (Clauses are called 'subordinate' because they do not make sense on their own and depend on the main clause.)

Main clause — *Joe laughed cheerfully at the joke, which made the others feel more relaxed.* — Subordinate clause

A **compound sentence** has two or more main clauses joined by a conjunction. Conjunctions are words such as *because*, *and*, *but*, *as*, *which* etc. In this case, both main clauses (underlined below) would make sense on their own.

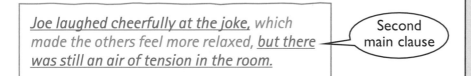

Joe laughed cheerfully at the joke, which made the others feel more relaxed, but there was still an air of tension in the room. — Second main clause

Rework these simple sentences yourself into complex and compound sentences:

(a) The bus was very late.

Complex sentence: _____

Compound sentence: _____

_____

(b) Granny glared irritably at the shop assistant.

Complex sentence: _____

Compound sentence: _____

_____

Answers and guidance are on page 112.

HINTS

Using the correct internal punctuation in compound and complex sentences is very important. Make sure you have punctuated your sentences correctly. Use these notes to help you.

- **Commas** make the meaning of a sentence clear by showing that one part is separate from another. They should be used before conjunctions and in lists. It is most important to use pairs of commas to mark subordinate clauses or phrases; this will help you to reach a higher level in your writing. For example:
Joe, the boy with the stammer, laughed cheerfully at the joke.

- **Semi-colons and colons** can be used to create different effects in your sentence structure. For example, instead of a conjunction, use a semi-colon:
Joe laughed at the joke; there was still an air of tension in the room.

- Or use a colon where there is a strong connection between what might be written as two smaller sentences:
Joe had a stammer: it made him feel different.

3 USE SENTENCE LENGTH TO CREATE AN EFFECT

Very short sentences, mixed with longer ones, are a skilful way to make an impact. Look at this example:

> **At last!** With a cheerful wave to her faithful friends, Nazra finally set off on the amazing journey she had spent months planning; all the time wondering if she would ever reach her goal. **She was jubilant.** Venturing into the unknown, Nazra's excitement grew with each flap of her newly acquired, brilliantly glittering, wings.

This technique:

* helps to stress a particular point;
* gives the reader time for a pause to think;
* shows that the writer is in control.

Several short sentences together can create a different sort of effect.

He listened. There was no sound. Nothing but silence. Peace.

It is difficult to read a series of short sentences quickly. The reader's pace has to change. The writer is in charge and has created a particular effect.

Try writing four very short sentences yourself about a car crash.

_____

_____

Now join the sentences together to make two longer ones.

_____

_____

Think about when it would be best to use each type of sentence structure.

4 UNDERSTAND HOW AND WHEN TO USE QUESTIONS AND EXCLAMATIONS

Questions can be used to draw your readers into your writing, especially when you are asking them to interact with you directly.

Complete these examples:

1 Do you know how many fleas _____
2 Have you ever thought about _____
3 What sort of person would _____

Using questions to draw readers in is a clever technique, but use it sparingly. Ask too many questions and it will sound as if you don't have the answers!

Exclamations help to emphasise a point. They too need to be used sparingly. Treat yourself to no more than two exclamations in any one piece of writing. And that's final!

Answers and guidance are on page 112.

Using speech in your writing develops characters and adds variety. However, you must use it with care and caution and know how to punctuate it.

Here are some guidelines that you need to remember when writing speech:

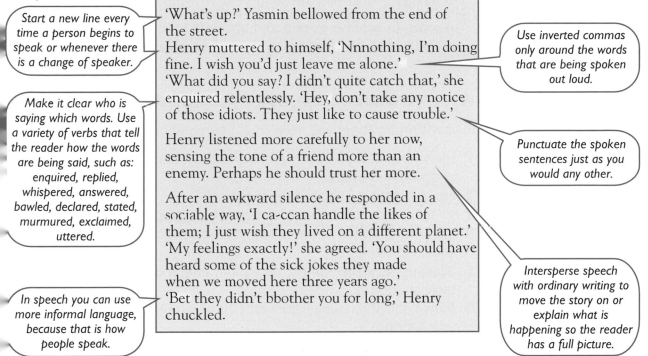

Start a new line every time a person begins to speak or whenever there is a change of speaker.

Make it clear who is saying which words. Use a variety of verbs that tell the reader how the words are being said, such as: enquired, replied, whispered, answered, bawled, declared, stated, murmured, exclaimed, uttered.

In speech you can use more informal language, because that is how people speak.

'What's up?' Yasmin bellowed from the end of the street.
Henry muttered to himself, 'Nnnothing, I'm doing fine. I wish you'd just leave me alone.'
'What did you say? I didn't quite catch that,' she enquired relentlessly. 'Hey, don't take any notice of those idiots. They just like to cause trouble.'

Henry listened more carefully to her now, sensing the tone of a friend more than an enemy. Perhaps he should trust her more.

After an awkward silence he responded in a sociable way, 'I ca-ccan handle the likes of them; I just wish they lived on a different planet.'
'My feelings exactly!' she agreed. 'You should have heard some of the sick jokes they made when we moved here three years ago.'
'Bet they didn't bbother you for long,' Henry chuckled.

Use inverted commas only around the words that are being spoken out loud.

Punctuate the spoken sentences just as you would any other.

Intersperse speech with ordinary writing to move the story on or explain what is happening so the reader has a full picture.

Continue the conversation above in the space below:

_____

_____

_____

_____

_____

HINTS

- When writing complex sentences, **use the correct internal punctuation**, particularly commas to mark clauses, or in pairs when giving additional information.
- If you have more than three **connectives** in a sentence, such as 'and', 'but', 'because', it probably needs reworking.
- Use as wide a range of punctuation marks as is necessary, particularly ones that create a deliberate effect.
- Remember that **variety is the key to success**. Don't overuse any of the sentence structure techniques suggested above or they will lose their impact.
- **Always leave enough time to check your punctuation.** Make changes if necessary and don't worry if it looks a little untidy.

Answers and guidance are on pages 112–113.

Paragraphs help you organise your ideas and they help readers to navigate their way through your writing.

In order to achieve level 5 and above in your Writing Paper, you will need to show that you can use paragraphs effectively.

WHY YOU NEED TO USE PARAGRAPHS

In your Writing Paper you need to use paragraphs to:

1 show obvious divisions in your writing, such as setting out speech or giving quotations;
2 group together similar ideas or topics;
3 signal a logical order, development of ideas or sequence of events;
4 gain the attention of the reader through effective introductions and conclusions;
5 indicate the subject of the paragraph that is to follow through topic sentences;
6 show control by using varied lengths of paragraphs to give pace to your writing;
7 give your writing an obviously organised structure through the links that help the reader to move from one paragraph to another.

These points are listed in order of difficulty. The further down the list you can go, the higher the level you will be able to achieve.

HOW GOOD ARE YOUR PARAGRAPHING SKILLS?

Begin by reviewing some of your writing in a variety of subjects. Then complete the chart below by putting a tick in the appropriate column:

Question	Always	Sometimes	Not very often
Is your writing paragraphed?			
Are the ideas in your paragraphs about the same topic?			
When you start a new paragraph, is it because you have changed topic?			
Do your paragraphs have a clear opening sentence that introduces the topic that follows?			
Do you begin and end with obvious introductions and conclusions?			
Do you use paragraphs of different lengths?			
Are your paragraphs carefully constructed so that they lead logically from one to another?			

Choose three areas where the ticks are not in the 'always' column, which you think you could improve on. Make a conscious effort to focus on these three areas.

HOW TO USE PARAGRAPHS WELL

Look at the way Nelson Mandela has used paragraphs in this extract from his autobiography, *Long Walk to Freedom.* Some features have been annotated to start you off. Continue the annotation by finding the others, listed below, for yourself:

1 New paragraph that marks the start of a different topic to the previous one.

2 Ideas contained within the paragraph are all to do with the same topic.

3 Varied paragraph length to add variety and pace.

4 Opening sentence to a paragraph that introduces the topic that follows.

5 Closing sentence that brings the topic of the paragraph to a close.

6 Closing sentence to a paragraph that leads the reader into the topic of the paragraph that follows.

7 Specific concluding sentence that 'rounds off' the passage and its theme.

Opening sentence introduces the topic of the passage.

My actual release time was set for 3 p.m. There were already dozens of people at the house, and the entire scene took on the aspect of a celebration. Warrant Officer Swart prepared a final meal for all of us and I thanked him not only for the food he had provided for the last two years but also for the companionship.

Opening paragraph sets the scene for the story that follows.

There was little time for lengthy farewells. I had told the authorities that I wanted to be able to say good-bye to the guards and warders who had looked after me and I asked that they and their families wait for me at the front gate, where I would be able to thank them individually.

By 3.30, I began to get restless, as we were already behind schedule. I told the members of the Reception Committee that my people had been waiting for me for twenty-seven years and I did not want to keep them waiting any longer. Shortly before four, we left in a small motorcade from the cottage. About a quarter of a mile in front of the gate, the car slowed to a stop and Winnie and I got out and began to walk towards the prison gate.

Opening sentence signals a change in topic.

At first I could not really make out what was going on in front of us but when I was within 150 feet or so, I saw a tremendous commotion and a great crowd of people: hundreds of photographers and television cameras and newspeople as well as several thousand well-wishers. I was astounded and a little bit alarmed. I had truly not expected such a scene; at most, I had imagined that there would be several dozen people. I realized we had not thoroughly prepared for what was about to happen.

Closing sentence draws paragraph to a close and indicates the next topic.

Within twenty feet or so of the gate, the cameras started clicking, a noise that sounded like some great herd of metallic beasts. Reporters started shouting questions; television crews began crowding in; ANC supporters were yelling and cheering. It was a happy, if slightly disorienting, chaos. When a television crew thrust a long, dark and furry object at me, I recoiled slightly, wondering if it were some newfangled weapon developed while I was in prison. Winnie informed me that it was a microphone.

When I was among the crowd I raised my right fist, and there was a roar. I had not been able to do that for twenty-seven years and it gave me a surge of strength and joy. As I finally walked through those gates to enter a car on the other side, I felt – even at the age of seventy-one – that my life was beginning anew. My ten thousand days of imprisonment were at last over.

Answers and guidance are on page 113.

ORGANISING YOUR PARAGRAPHS FOR DIFFERENT TASKS AND TEXT TYPES

Different types of tasks and texts need to be organised and structured in different ways. The order and organisation of your paragraphs need to show this.

Revising some skeleton structures and outlines will save time in your Test.

Copy out on a sheet of paper the three writing 'skeletons' below and complete the planning suggested in each task.

1   Recount – such as telling a story or relating a personal experience, where your structure is ordered according to time. Think of each horizontal line as a new paragraph. (Add more arrows/paragraphs if you think you will need them.)

TASK
Write about what happened on a school or family trip to an adventure park.

opening paragraph –
(where you went, when and why)

paragraph 2 –

paragraph 3 –

paragraph 4 –

concluding paragraph –
(reaching home, final thoughts about the day)

2   Discussion – In this type of writing you need to consider arguments from different points of view. You may be asked to write a newspaper or magazine article, or consider a topical issue in an essay in response to a question such as: 'Should any country be allowed to hunt whales?'

Some points have been given on the skeleton as illustrations to start you off.

Introducing the topic in general:

TASK
Write an article for a teenage magazine on the topic: 'Should homework be set for pupils in year 8 and below?'

Reasons for	**Reasons against**
★ good preparation for future	★ can learn how to study when older
★ creates more learning time	★ should be enough time in lessons
★	★
★	★
★	★

Conclusion: drawing together points raised

3 Persuasion – the purpose of this type of writing is to influence or convince others to adopt a particular point of view. It could include writing a newspaper or magazine article, a travel brochure or a pamphlet for a pressure group like Greenpeace.

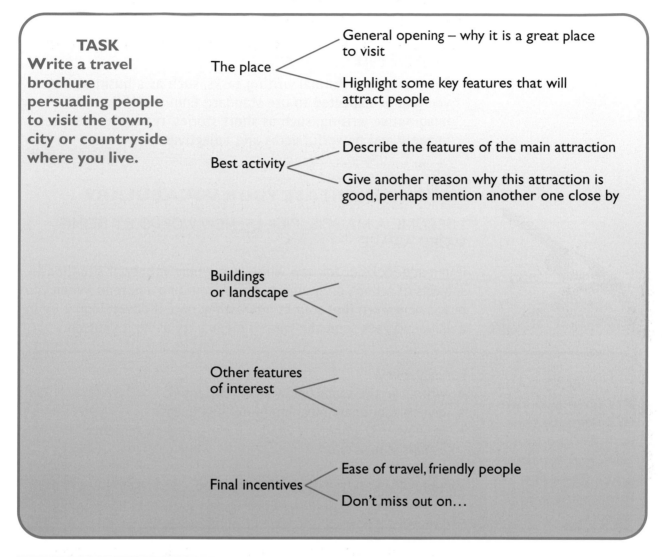

TASK
Write a travel brochure persuading people to visit the town, city or countryside where you live.

The place
- General opening – why it is a great place to visit
- Highlight some key features that will attract people

Best activity
- Describe the features of the main attraction
- Give another reason why this attraction is good, perhaps mention another one close by

Buildings or landscape

Other features of interest

Final incentives
- Ease of travel, friendly people
- Don't miss out on…

HINTS
You will feel under pressure because of the time limit in your Test, but you must:
- understand the **type of writing** you have been asked to complete;
- remember how this writing type should be **structured**;
- **organise the order** of your paragraphs before you begin to write;
- **plan your paragraphs** – content and style;
- bring your writing to a **conclusion**.

Improving your vocabulary and expression

Examiners will look specifically at your vocabulary: its range and suitability for the task.

For example, in formal writing tasks, such as a business letter, you will be expected to use standard English. With more imaginative writing, such as short stories, readers will expect imagery and powerful verbs and adjectives.

WAYS TO INCREASE YOUR VOCABULARY

1 BECOME A MAGPIE: PICK UP NEW WORDS BY BEING 'WORD AWARE'

Listen and look out for new words in a whole variety of situations – subjects at school, programmes on TV, anything you read. When you hear a new word that sounds interesting, note it down; look it up in a dictionary; ask someone what it means; try using it yourself.

TASK
You have two days to complete this task. Follow the advice given above and collect five interesting new words.

For each one:
• write it in the space below (spelt correctly);
• give its dictionary meaning (don't just guess);
• to show that you know what it means, write a sentence using the new word.

Word:	Meaning:

Sentence: _____

Word:	Meaning:

Sentence: _____

Word:	Meaning:

Sentence: _____

Word:	Meaning:

Sentence: _____

Word:	Meaning:

Sentence: _____

2 HOOK UP TO A THESAURUS, EITHER IN BOOK FORM OR ON THE COMPUTER

A thesaurus gives you more interesting words that you might be able to use instead of a dull, overused word. For example, here are some of the alternatives that the Collins Thesaurus gives for 'walk':

amble, hike, march, saunter, stride, stroll, traipse, tramp, trudge

Don't expect that every word given to you as an alternative can be used in place of the one you have just looked up. You need to test out the alternatives to make sure that they really do fit.

TASK 1
A thesaurus has provided alternatives to some of the words used in this extract. Underline the one that you think would be the best replacement.

Every day seemed hotter than the last in the small Cambodian village. The parched land was scorched and even the weeds on it had withered. The water in the river that meandered through the fields was almost all gone. The riverbed lay cracked into smooth brown clay tiles. The sky, no longer blue, glared a painful yellow. The sun was hidden by dust.

small: tiny diminutive unimportant little miniature
land: ground territory place soil earth
fields: countryside territory grassland area meadows
brown: chocolate russet brunette bronzed tanned
painful: throbbing anguished excruciating burning agonizing

TASK 2
Pick out five words from this extract and use a thesaurus to find a more interesting replacement.

The country needs farming to help its people to live. Farming also gives the people a good source of raw material to help the country's industry and it also helps to bring in cash from other countries. Unfortunately water shortages have a bad effect on farming. Food can become scarce, especially in dry areas where the people depend on irrigation to supply their valuable water.

1 Word from the extract: Replacement:

2 Word from the extract: Replacement:

3 Word from the extract: Replacement:

4 Word from the extract: Replacement:

5 Word from the extract: Replacement:

HINTS
Using a wider vocabulary is important because it:
- helps you avoid repetition;
- makes your writing more interesting;
- allows you to choose more appropriate words;
- enables you to be more precise.

Answers and guidance are on page 113.

3 CHECK YOUR EXPRESSION AND TONE

Make sure that the language you use suits the form and purpose of your writing. There are occasions where too formal a tone is unsuitable. You also need to consider the likely age of your intended readers.

Look at the vocabulary and expression in the following extracts. Circle the words and phrases where you think the writer has used inappropriate language. Add your suggestions as annotations at the side. Then rewrite the extracts in a more appropriate style.

TASK A

Purpose: to explain the term 'endangered species'
Intended readers: children aged 9–10 years old
Form: a leaflet encouraging young people to learn more about caring for the environment

What is an 'endangered species'?

Flora and fauna that are in jeopardy may be classified as 'endangered' if they run the risk of extinction by fulfilling certain criteria. The species in question must be:

- declining in numbers;
- confined to a small, possibly fragmented population;
- occur in only a small region;
- liable to become extinct within a specified time.

Some susceptible species are less severely threatened, but they are constantly at risk if they lose their remaining habitat.

Children can contribute to the protection of such vulnerable organisms by gaining an enduring awareness of the consequences that will follow the destruction of significant areas of the planet.

_____

_____

_____

_____

_____

_____

_____

Answers and guidance are on page 113.

TASK B
Purpose: to give information about the history of the melon
Intended readers: adults/gardeners
Form: a gardening encyclopaedia

Melons: In England we are just beginning to try our hand at growing melons, but did you know they have been grown in France for ages? In fact no one actually knows exactly how long. The first crystal-clear date that we have on record is roundabout 1495, when, rumour has it, King Charles VIII smuggled in some seeds following a jaunt visiting the pope in Italy. Those popes certainly chomped their way through a lot of melons, even tho' they were then mega expensive. Word is that one greedy glutton, Pope Paul II, actually died of gorging himself on them in 1471.

HINTS
- **You will not be able to use a dictionary or a thesaurus in your Test,** but training yourself to use them beforehand will help raise your awareness about words in general.
- In your Test, read through your work and look for places where using a more interesting or more exact word would be better. **Make changes and don't worry if it looks a little untidy.** You will in fact be given credit for demonstrating your editing skills.
- Remember, **it is always better to use a higher-level word, rather than an ordinary one, even if you are not sure of the spelling.** You gain more credit for an interesting, unusual or more exact word, even if incorrectly spelt, than for a correctly spelt ordinary word.
- Always take care to **match your vocabulary, tone and expression to the task and intended audience.** But be careful, never let your expression become too informal in a Test.

Answers and guidance are on page 114.

Gaining confidence with spelling

Some marks for the shorter writing task on the Writing Paper are allocated to spelling, but many more marks are given to the way you write and what you have to say.

Nevertheless, taking care with your spelling will help you communicate clearly and avoid confusion.

WAYS TO IMPROVE YOUR SPELLING

One of the best ways to improve your spelling is to know where your greatest weaknesses lie. Which words are most likely to catch you out? You can be forgiven for not being able to spell unusual or difficult words, such as *trepidation* or *ventriloquist*, but you ought to be able to manage words such as *because*, *disappear* or *necessary*.

STEP 1 ATTACK YOUR OWN 'DANGER POINTS'

Everyone has words that they know are trouble. The trick is to make a real effort to master these words and find a way of making sure you remember them once and for all!

1 Look through your written work in several subjects.
2 Make a list of your common mistakes.
3 Leave aside specialist words related only to a particular subject.
4 Write your 'top ten' most common errors of everyday words in the boxes on the left.

Choose five of these words and for each one invent a 'mnemonic'.

A mnemonic works like this:
• for each letter, choose a word that begins with that letter;
• make the words you choose into a memorable phrase;
• remember the saying, and you will remember how to spell the word.

Here's an example. Add your own in the other boxes.

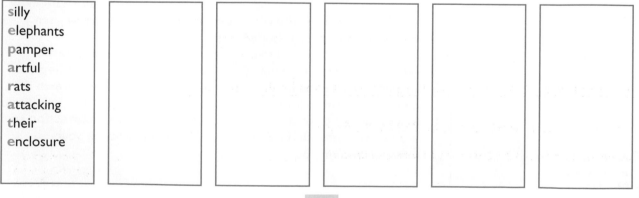

silly
elephants
pamper
artful
rats
attacking
their
enclosure

STEP 2 LEARN HOW TO CHANGE THE END OF A WORD

Changing the end of a word by adding 'ing', 'ed' or making a word plural often leads to spelling mistakes.

Changing verbs by adding 'ing' or 'ed':
- Most words just add 'ing' or 'ed'.
- Some words drop the last letter 'e' before adding 'ing'.
- A few words, those with a short vowel sound, double the last letter before adding 'ing' or 'ed'.

Add 'ing'/'ed' to these words and put them in the correct column. Underline the exceptions.

> **NOTE**
> There are some exceptions in making the past tense, where, rather than adding 'ed', a new word is created, e.g. *fight, fighting, fought.*

drip	travel	donate	buy	watch	succeed	meet
decide	come	swim	write	chop	begin	enjoy

Just add 'ing' or 'ed'	**Drop last letter 'e'**	**Double last letter**
catching / caught	hoping / hoped	running / ran

Making plurals – more than one

There are two common ways of making plurals.

> **NOTE**
> There are some words such as *oxen, roofs* that break the rule.

1. By adding 's' to the word, e.g. *book – books*
2. By adding 'es' to the word, for example:
   - words that end in **x** or **z** add 'es', e.g. *boxes, buzzes*
   - words that end in **ch** or **sh** add 'es', e.g. *branches, dishes*
   - words that end in **s** or **o** add 'es', e.g. *glasses, heroes*
   - words that end in **f** change to 'ves', e.g. *halves, calves*

Use these guidelines to write the plural of the words below:

wish		wolf		hairbrush	
mass		address		leaf	
tax		volcano		loaf	
tomato		witch		sandwich	

Some words have different rules. Look at the groups of words below and write the rule that applies to them when changing from singular (one) to plural.

| keys | donkeys | days | boys | **BUT** | pennies | armies | cities | parties |

The rule is: when a word has a vowel before the final 'y' _____

But when a word has a consonant before the final 'y' _____

Answers and guidance are on page 114.

ADDING A PREFIX – a group of letters added to the beginning of a word

Adding a prefix to a word changes its meaning. For example:
- If you add 'un' or 'dis' to a word it makes it mean the opposite, e.g. *unkind* means 'not kind', *distrust* means 'you do not trust'.
- If you add 're' to a word it means 'again', e.g. *redo* means 'do again'.

How many new words can you make from those given below by adding 'un', 'dis' or 're'? Make a list and put the new words into the correct column below. Remember, it may be possible to add more than one prefix to some of the words.

allow	appear	build	order	satisfactory
happy	play	fair	organise	qualify
visit	honest	comfort	continue	wind

Adding 'un'	Adding 'dis'	Adding 're'

ADDING A SUFFIX – letters added to the end of a word

Like a prefix, a suffix changes the meaning of the original word, e.g.:
- 'ful' means 'full of', as in *careful*
- 'less' means 'without', as in *careless*
- 'able' means 'able to', as in *readable*

Create new words by adding the suffix 'able', 'less' or 'ful' to the words below and write them in the correct column. It is possible to add more than one prefix to some words, e.g. *thankful* and *thankless*.

hope	mercy	respect	break	thank
success	forget	colour	duty	avoid
beauty	grace	enjoy	thought	fear

Words ending in 'ful'	Words ending in 'less'	Words ending in 'able'

NOTE
When a suffix is added to words ending with a consonant before the 'y', the 'y' changes into an 'i' before the suffix is added, for example **pity** becomes **pitiful**.

STEP 4 USE RHYMING TO HELP YOU TO SPELL WORDS THAT SOUND THE SAME

Groups of letters often found together, such as *ough* and *ight*, are called 'strings'.

- Some words that end in the same letter string rhyme, e.g., *sight* and *light*.
- Some words that end with the same letter string sound very different, such as *plough* and *tough*.
- Some words rhyme but don't have the same letter string, e.g. *night* and *write*.

In the box below write as many words as you can that use these letter strings:

'ight'	'ough'	'ear'
tonight	through	learn

STEP 5 GET TO KNOW YOUR WORD FAMILIES

Words that have a common root or stem, such as *create*, *creation*, *creative*, *creator*, belong to a 'word family'. Knowing this can help you to spell; if you can spell one word in the family, it will help you to spell the others too. For example:

- Verbs can be made from nouns and adjectives by adding suffixes such as 'ify', and 'ise': *horror/horrify*, *apology/apologise*.
- Verbs that end in 'ate' come from the same word root as nouns that end in 'tion', for example *dictate/dictation*, *celebrate/celebration*.
- Verbs ending in 'en' are linked in a similar way with adjectives such as *weak* and *weaken*, *sad* and *sadden*.

How many words, belonging to the same word family, can you make from these 'root' words? Use your dictionary to check your answers.

> ### HINTS
> In your Test remember:
> - You may not think you are a good speller, but **taking greater care** will help.
> - Leave time to **check through your writing** and correct any errors you find.
> - Use words that you know you can spell, but remember that **showing you have a wide vocabulary** is also very important.

motivate	
purify	
indicate	
illustrate	
dream	
classify	
quicken	

The examiners will be assessing your general communication skills, as well as your ability to engage the interest of an audience.

It is therefore very important that you spend time planning what you are going to write – and checking through what you have written.

In your Test, you will not have time to draft your work, but in the Writing Paper there will be a planning sheet linked specifically with the longer writing task – USE IT!

Below is an example of a writing task. The student has started the planning, but you need to complete the notes. Take about 5 minutes.

LONGER WRITING TASK:
On the streets

You should spend about 45 minutes writing and 15 minutes planning.

While exploring a strange city on a school trip, a teenager becomes confused and cannot find the way back to the rest of his/her group.

Tell the story of what happens.

Remember that in telling the story you will need to:
- decide on a setting
- create a central character
- narrate events, including a complication
- provide a resolution

PLANNING

What is the setting for the story?
- Paris – near the river
-
-

Who is the central character?
- 13-year-old boy
-
-

What happens?
- Looking at boats unloading produce for the market – then his group has gone
-
-

Complication
- A woman accuses him of stealing her purse
-
-

How is the situation resolved?
- Police called
-
-

CHECKING YOUR WORK

Make sure you leave time to check your work through once you have finished writing. Examiners will give you credit for editing your work and showing that you are aware of how it could be improved. Don't worry if it looks a little untidy because of the changes you have made.

Read the extract below, which is taken from a student's response to the task on the previous page. Imagine you are the student checking through your work. What changes or corrections would you make?

Write on the passage itself to show the changes, just as you would do in the actual Test.

...Suddenly Chris didn't know were to turn. The streets all looked the same and the buildings towared above him. He tries to look at his map, but the writing was too small and in any case the words seemed so strange he couldn't hold them in his head. The noise around him was increasing. People were calling out prices gossipping in corners and their was a busker hammering out a tune somewhere in the distance. What should he do? Where should he go. I decided to try again and see if someone spoke any English. He went to a flower stand a little apart from the others on the edge by the water.

In spite of all the confusion he felt within himself, Chris couldn't help noticing the chearful colours of the flowers – reds and blues, whites and yellows – dancing in the sun light. For a moment he stood looking at them, forgetting his troubles. Suddenly there was a shout from the woman next to him. She started shouting something in French and he didn't understand what she was saying, but it didn't sound very pleasant and she kept point at him and shaking her finger...

HINTS
- Spend about 15 minutes reading the question and planning before you start to write.
- Refer to your plan when you are writing.
- It doesn't matter if you make changes whilst you are writing, the planning sheet is not marked.
- Leave at least 3 minutes to read through and check your work.
- Make sure any changes you make are clear.

Answers and guidance are on pages 114–115.

Using your imagination to create characters

The longer writing task on your Writing Paper could well involve imaginative or personal writing. You may be asked to create a story around a given situation, recount a personal experience or explore a theme in an imaginative way.

Gaining the attention of your audience, and using your imaginative powers, even when writing about a true event, are essential.

The task that you have already planned in Revision session 5, pages 38–39, will now provide a starting point for your writing in this one.

HOW TO CREATE BELIEVABLE CHARACTERS

Characters are central to any story. Creating people that your reader can understand, and feel something for, is important. Remember this advice:

- Picture the people in your story clearly in your head before you start to write – even if one of them is yourself!
- Base your characters on real people. It is best to write about what you know, even if the character is an imaginary mix of several different 'real' people.
- Be consistent. Don't change the way a person thinks, talks or reacts halfway through the story, unless something has happened to change them.
- Create interest in your characters. Make your readers care about what happens to them, so they will read on.

Look at your notes on the central character that you created on page 38. You will need to bring this person to life in your story and make your readers want to read about him/her.

HOW DO WRITERS CREATE CHARACTERS?

Write your ideas below. Characters are created by:

Answers and guidance are on page 115.

DESCRIBING A CHARACTER

It is natural to want to give some idea of what your characters look like, their age, the way they dress and so on during the course of your story. Details like this help your reader to 'see' the people in your story. Avoid the temptation to do this at the very beginning, or all at once. It is enough to give indications here and there as you go along – you don't need to give a whole life history!

Imagine the boy in your story and the woman whose purse has been stolen. Write a few notes about them in the columns below:

Details	Boy	Woman
Age		
Facial features – eyes, hair etc.		
Clothes they wear		
Height		
Other points		

Choose two of these points and include them in a sentence on each character on a separate piece of paper.

CREATING A PERSON THROUGH THEIR THOUGHTS AND ACTIONS

In your story you need to show not only what characters do, but also what they think. Go back to the boy in your story. The way in which you choose to portray him when he first discovers he has been left behind by his group will help to create his character. For example, does he rush around looking for his friends or does he stand still in fear? Does he panic inwardly or does he think a great opportunity has just presented itself? Write your ideas below:

What does he do when he first discovers that he has been left behind by his group?	
What does he think about his situation?	

Write two sentences for each of these on a separate piece of paper.

As you write your story, continue to think about the character notes that you made here and use them to inform the way in which your character thinks and acts, in particular when the crisis arises and in the final resolution.

Other ways to create characters, through what they say and what others say about them, will be covered on pages 46–47.

HINTS
- Introduce the characters in your story in a **natural** way.
- **Avoid** giving a life history – readers don't need to know everything.
- **Never** begin 'My name is' or 'This story is about a fourteen-year-old boy named ...'
- **Rework blunt statements.** For example, 'Chris was a shy, quiet boy' could become: 'Chris, always a little shy, quietly asked the way ...'

Answers and guidance are on pages 115–116.

Structuring beginnings and endings

The first paragraph of your writing is crucial to gaining the interest and attention of your audience. This always makes it the most difficult to write! There are approaches that will help you, though.

MAKING AN IMPRESSIVE START

Look at these four opening paragraphs and put them in order of merit (1 being the best):

Order	
	Extract 1 Have you ever had the eerie feeling that something is not quite right? That was how Chris felt when he realised that, although surrounded by people, he was, in fact, alone. The vibrant market had fascinated him, but it had also lured him into a trap. His school party had moved on. He had been deserted.
	Extract 2 Chris got up early that morning because he was looking forward to the trip to Paris, which was part of the school's foreign exchange trip to France. He had always wanted to visit this famous city. He chatted to his friend on the coach and they both decided that it was going to be a fun day.
	Extract 3 'Where is everyone?' Looking around the bright market place, Chris suddenly realised he was alone. His school friends had all disappeared. He looked about in panic and could only hear strange, foreign-sounding words he could not understand. What should he do now?
	Extract 4 Crimson. Indigo. Emerald. Colours fluttered all around him as the market traders began creating their magical scene. Sucked into their midst, Chris was absorbed by the strange sounds and exotic smells. Gradually it dawned on him that something was wrong. He appeared to have been abandoned in this unfamiliar place.

Now see which of these extracts follows the advice below. Against each suggestion write the numbers of the extracts that have used this approach.

TASK A
Use the advice given above to write your own opening paragraph to the story set on page 38.

Capture the interest of the reader by:	
Starting at a significant point that creates an immediate impact	
Creating a sense of mystery that makes the reader want to read on	
Using an interesting variety of words that sound appealing	
Making the subject of your writing clear in the first few sentences	
Varying the length of your sentences to create an effect	
Beginning with a conversation that generates interest in a situation	
Having an unusual approach that will intrigue the reader	
Acknowledging the reader in some way, such as asking a question	

Answers and guidance are on pages 116–117.

CREATING A SUCCESSFUL ENDING

Bringing your writing to a successful ending is very important. Watch the clock and make sure that you allow yourself enough time, at least 5 minutes, to bring your writing to a real conclusion. There is nothing worse than having to put your pen down before you have really finished.

Let's go back to Chris, lost in Paris. If you were a reader, what would you most want to know about what happens to him at the end of the story? Write three more questions below (the most obvious one has been done for you).

1 <u>Does he find his school group again?</u>

2 _____

3 _____

4 _____

Answers and guidance are on page 117.

Some of these questions may have been answered before the final paragraph, but you need to save something 'special' for the very end. Here are some suggestions:

1 A 'twist in the tale', perhaps ending with a question, is effective as it takes the reader by surprise. Just when they thought it was all over, you tell them something unexpected.
2 The narrator addresses the reader directly, perhaps giving them a piece of advice arising from your story, making them feel included.
3 Introduce a mystery, something that is unresolved so the reader is given something to think about when they have finished reading.
4 Unhappy or sad endings tend to be more interesting than happy ones, but don't overdo it!

TASK B
Choose one of these ending types. Write the conclusion that best matches the introduction to the story that you wrote for the task on page 38.

Now look back at the opening paragraphs opposite. Match each of the endings to an appropriate beginning. (Style is a clue too.)

Type		Extract
4	Although he was glad to be back with his friends, Chris was sorry he had caused so much fuss. Perhaps if he hadn't got lost, the old woman wouldn't have ended up in the hospital that day. It was all his fault.	
3	The image of the old woman haunted Chris as he closed his eyes that night. What were the strange words she had whispered to him as he was taken away? Then, softly murmuring in his head, he heard a voice, 'You are the one. You know you are the one.' And he knew it was something he would never be able to forget.	
2	Despite all that had happened, Chris was glad he had been lost. The experience had taught him something new about himself and other people. So if ever you find yourself deserted in a strange place, don't despair, maybe you too, like Chris, will emerge a wiser human being as a result.	
1	Aching limbs. Empty, growling stomach. Chris stared vacantly. The sky, just dawning, lit the tops of towering buildings. How had he got here? Was his mind playing tricks on him? Was this real?	

43 FOCUS ON WRITING

Choosing a narrative voice and exploring personal feelings

In some writing tasks that are set in the Test, you will be directed to write from a certain perspective such as 'tell your story', indicating a first-person story from a personal perspective, or it may be left open for you to choose.

NARRATIVE VOICE AND PERSPECTIVE

narrator – someone who tells a story.

narrative voice – the 'person' the writer uses to tell a story, which can be first person ('I') or third person ('he' or 'she'). Sometimes the narrative voice is an 'all-seeing' narrator who speaks independently as the story is told.

narrative perspective – the point of view from which a story is written. For example, a first-person story could be written from the point of view of an imaginary character or the writer herself/himself; a third-person story could focus on the thoughts and feelings of a particular character or different characters at different times.

Before you begin to write, you must decide on the voice and narrative perspective. The most common options are given below. Comment on the advantages and disadvantages of each.

Narrative voice	Narrative perspective	Advantages	Disadvantages
First person (I)	told by yourself as yourself	• You know what really happened	• You don't really know what other people felt
First person (I)	told by a character you have created		
Third person (he or she)	narrator who makes comments and addresses the reader directly		
Third person (he or she)	simply telling the story in the past tense		

HINTS

• If you are given a choice, write in **the voice** that you feel comfortable with.
• Once you have started writing in a particular voice, **don't change** part way through. For example, if the story is in the third person don't suddenly say, 'I thought ...'

Answers and guidance are on page 118.

EXPERIENCES AND FEELINGS

Whatever narrative voice or perspective you choose, you will need to write in a personal way about experiences and feelings, real or imaginary. Exploring how people feel about experiences or situations creates interest and provides insight into characters.

Let's return to Chris, who has discovered that he has been left behind on the streets of Paris. How do you think he feels? One way to approach the question is to ask yourself: 'How would I feel if I was in his situation?'

In the box below, add at least five words that could be used to describe the feelings you think Chris might experience on discovering he is on his own. Be as inventive and imaginative as you can – the obvious ones are there already.

Answers and guidance are on page 119.

> afraid   panic   excited

Relating the feelings of your characters to yourself helps to add realism, and it is good to write about what you know. However, imagining unusual or different feelings can add greater interest. For example, Chris might feel exhilarated at being on his own at last. He may feel that he has suddenly been given an opportunity to take part in a new adventure!

Write a short paragraph describing how Chris feels when he discovers he really is on his own. Remember, it must be from a third-person perspective.

_____

_____

_____

_____

Of course, it is not always necessary to write a whole paragraph. You can add comments, phrases or sentences about how the character is feeling as the action develops.

A valuable short-hand way of indicating feelings is to use adverbs, e.g.

> _Reluctantly_, using his very basic French, Chris decided to ask someone if they had seen a group of English students. He _nervously_ approached the busker on the edge of the square.

Adverbs to describe feelings

These two adverbs tell us about how the character felt. Write five more adverbs that describe feelings in the box on the right.

Writing entertaining dialogue

> We can learn a great deal about characters from what they say and what others say about them. Adding dialogue to your writing will create interest for your reader and may earn you extra marks.

When you are writing speech, remember these 'golden rules':

1 Use dialogue sparingly, in **short sharp bursts** – about a quarter of a page is the maximum length at any one time.

2 Correctly **punctuate** conversation (see page 25).

3 Clearly **identify each speaker**. Having two or three speakers works best; more becomes confusing.

4 **Write realistically**, using words that people really would say, including informal expressions.

5 Indicate **how the characters say their words** (adverbs) and/or **how they are feeling**.

How successful is the extract below at following the 'golden rules'?
- Find at least one example where you think the writer has followed each of the rules. Write the number of the rule alongside the example, in the left-hand margin.

Answers and guidance are on pages 119–120.

- What would your reader learn about Chris from reading this conversation?

Finally Chris found someone who could speak good English, a student who said she was studying English at University.

'One minute I was exploring the market, with my mates,' he explained calmly, 'and the next I was on my own.'

The student looked concerned. 'Where was your group going to next?' she asked.

Feeling a little foolish, Chris replied, 'It sounds daft, but I don't know. I was having a quiet kip when we were given the itinerary this morning on the coach.'

'What is a kip?' she enquired. 'That's a new word for me.'

'A kip is a snooze, a catnap, a doze, you know – forty winks and all that,' he teased. 'Only I wish I hadn't been having one this morning, or I wouldn't be in this mess now.'

The young woman looked desperately at her watch. 'I'm really sorry,' she gasped, 'but I've got to go now or I'll miss my driving lesson. Here's my mobile number, ring me if you don't have any luck finding your friends.'

She handed Chris a scrap of paper and disappeared into the crowded street.

Now it's your turn to write a conversation between Chris and a French policeman who thinks he is acting suspiciously. The policeman can speak English, but not perfectly.

Remember to follow the golden rules!

_____

_____

_____

_____

_____

_____

_____

_____

_____

_____

_____

_____

_____

_____

What would your reader gain from reading this conversation?

1 _____

2 _____

3 _____

4 _____

TASK
- Now it is time for you to write the complete story given on page 38.
- Start from the planning stage.
- Begin again from scratch if you prefer.
- If you like, give yourself 15 minutes to plan and 45 minutes to write. Time yourself to make it like a 'trial test'.

HINTS
- It is worth spending time creating an **impressive opening paragraph**.
- Make sure you can maintain the **same style** you start with.
- If you have the option, choose a **narrative voice** that suits you.
- **A strongly created character** will hold the interest of your reader.
- Describing how characters **feel** is important.
- **Conversation** is tricky, but worthwhile, especially when it entertains your reader.
- Make the effort to bring your writing to a well-thought-out, **definite conclusion**.

Answers and guidance are on pages 120–122.

In your Test you may be asked to produce a piece of writing that gives information. For example, you may be asked to write a report for a magazine or a newspaper, a tourist guidebook entry or a leaflet.

WHAT ARE THE FEATURES OF THIS TYPE OF WRITING?

Information text: Language features

- Present tense (unless writing about something that has already happened)
- Third person
- Factual writing
- Impersonal nouns and pronouns
- Often limited space requiring concise style that is to the point or in note form

Information text: Structure

- Information introducing topic, e.g. – who, what, when, where
- Non-chronological organisation (unless reporting events)
- Description additional to information
- Single topic

Answers and guidance are on page 123.

Annotate the text below by labelling the features you recognise from the boxes above. Some have already been done to start you off.

Who

Where

When

No Briton has ever started a world road race championship as the overwhelming favourite, but that is the status Nicole Cooke will enjoy in Monsanto Park this morning when she defends the women's junior title she won last year in Brittany.

'Enjoy' is perhaps not the most appropriate word: Cooke will be a heavily marked woman. The rest of the 64-rider field know full well that her back wheel is the best one to follow, and that if they can stay in her slipstream to the finish they may stand a chance of winning the gold medal.

Surprise is a key weapon in a road race but it is no longer part of Cooke's armoury. Since she sprinted across the line in Plouay in October with a yell of delight to become Britain's first ever junior road race champion, male or female, she has added the mountain-bike title and, on Tuesday, the time-trial gold.

SHORTER WRITING TASK

Write an article of between three and four paragraphs for the school brochure about the sports curriculum that is taken by year 9 students at your school.

You should spend about 30 minutes on this task.

Sports for year 9 students

Select appropriate information about some of the following:

★ length and frequency of PE lessons

★ sports facilities (e.g. swimming pool, gym, cricket pitch etc.)

★ opportunities for after-school clubs

★ competitive inter-school sports teams

★ seasonal variations

★ gender issues (e.g. Are boys and girls separated for PE? Do they have different activities? etc.)

★ sports kit and uniform requirements

PLANNING

Use the text skeleton below to help you plan and structure your writing. When you have finished, write your article on a separate piece of paper.

Answers and guidance are on page 123.

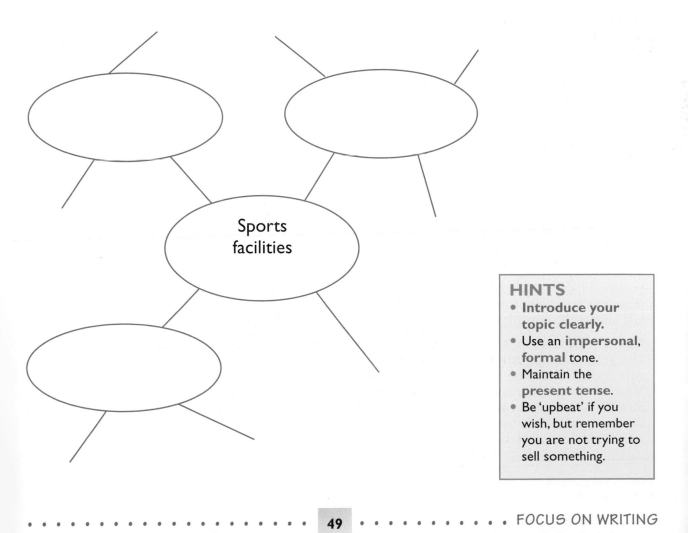

Sports facilities

HINTS
• Introduce your topic clearly.
• Use an **impersonal, formal** tone.
• Maintain the **present tense**.
• Be 'upbeat' if you wish, but remember you are not trying to sell something.

Writing to explain

The purpose of 'writing to explain' is to give details about how something happens, and to show the relationship between cause and effect.

Writing up a scientific experiment, questions and answers in a leaflet about health and safety, geographical details about the rain cycle are all examples of explanation texts.

WHAT ARE THE FEATURES OF THIS TYPE OF TEXT?

Explanation text: Language features

- Present tense
- Impersonal voice
- Time connectives such as 'first', 'then', 'after', plus other ways of showing a sequence of events such as diagrams
- Causal connectives such as 'when', 'therefore', 'if', 'because', 'in order to'
- Technical terminology, which is sometimes explained, for example: 'hydrogen, the lightest of all known gases'
- Sentences often complex

Explanation text: Structure

- Title tells reader the topic that is going to be explained or may ask a question, such as 'Why does rain fall?'
- Begins with general statements to introduce the topic
- Contains a series of logical steps explaining the process
- Usually uses a step-by-step order
- Often accompanied by diagrams
- Paragraphs indicate significant stages

Identify the features of an explanation text that you can find in this passage about gears. Some have been highlighted to start you off.

Gear Design

Some advantages of using gears to transmit forces, rather than other methods, include their small size and their ability to transmit large powers. On the other hand, gears are relatively expensive to make and require careful lubrication and protection from dirt.

How Do Gears Work?

One gear, called the driver, is meshed together with another, called the follower. When the driver is turned, the follower turns also. If the driver has 30 teeth, and the follower 60 teeth, then each time the driver turns twice the follower will turn only once. This means that the follower will turn at half the rate of the driver. The ratio between the speeds of the two wheels is called the velocity ratio. In this case the velocity ratio is 2. A velocity ratio greater than 1 means that a smaller effort at the input (the driver) can drive a larger load at the output (the follower), and the gears have a mechanical advantage.

When two gears are connected directly, the shafts rotate in opposite directions. A third wheel in the middle has no effect upon the overall velocity ratio, but causes the direction of rotation of the driven shaft to be reversed.

Answers and guidance are on page 124.

What is conservation?

Use the suggestions below as well as your own ideas.

What is conservation?

Human activities that harm the environment can be controlled or prevented through careful management of the earth's natural resources. This is called conservation. For example, governments can enforce new laws to control overfishing or deforestation. Pollution can be reduced by controlling the use of pesticides and fertilisers used in farming. Individuals can help by recycling products that use natural resources, such as paper, glass, plastic and metal.

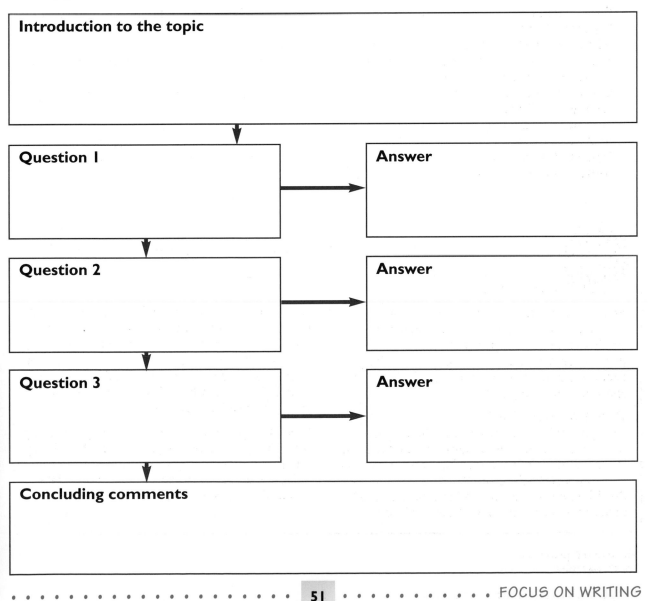

Introduction to the topic

Question 1	**Answer**
Question 2	**Answer**
Question 3	**Answer**

Concluding comments

Good descriptive writing can improve almost any writing task, whether it is factual or imaginative. It adds interest and detail that will help to engage the reader.

Descriptive writing may use powerful nouns and verbs, expressive adjectives and adverbs. You may want to include figurative language, such as metaphors and similes.

Compare the two passages below. The first is an account of coming across a group of penguins in the desert, where all forms of interesting description have been removed.

Ahead of us the vegetation stopped, and in its place was sand. This was separated from the sea by dunes. It was in this desert area that the penguins had made their nests. Among these holes were a lot of penguins. Most of the birds were adult; but each burrow contained two youngsters, without their feathers, which looked at us. The adults had wattles round the base of their beaks and eyes.

Here is the same passage as it was originally written by Gerald Durrell in *The Whispering Land*, complete with his own particular brand of imaginative description.

- Underline all the powerful nouns and verbs.
- Highlight the adjectives and adverbs.
- Annotate all the examples of figurative language, such as metaphors and similes, that you can find.

Ahead of us the low, brown scrub petered out, and in its place was a great desert of sun-cracked sand. This was separated from the sea beyond by crescent-shaped white sand dunes, very steep and some two-hundred feet high. It was in this desert area protected from the sea that the penguins had created their *city*. … In among these craters waddled the biggest collection of penguins I had ever seen, *like a sea of pigmy headwaiters*, solemnly shuffling to and fro as if suffering from fallen arches due to a lifetime of carrying overloaded trays. Their numbers were so prodigious, stretching to the furthermost horizon where they twinkled black and white in the heat haze. …

The greater proportion of birds were, of course, adult; but each nesting burrow contained two youngsters, still wearing their baby coats of down, who regarded us with big, melting dark eyes, looking like plump, shy debutantes clad in outsized silver-fox furs. The adults, sleek and neat in their black and white suits, had red wattles round the base of their beaks, and bright, predatory, street peddler eyes.

From Gerald Durrell, *The Whispering Land*, pages 46–47

Simile links with ocean, creating image of numbers and size of penguins

Metapho[r] give the impressi[on] of the siz[e] and organisat[ion] of the penguin commun[ity]

Answers and guidance are on page 125.

HOW TO CREATE YOUR OWN DESCRIPTIVE LANGUAGE

Follow these simple steps:

1 At a simple level, you can use **adjectives** to describe: the *enormous* tree

2 To create an image, compare it with something else: *a bent and twisted witch*

3 Put the two together to create a **simile**: the enormous tree stood black against the sky *like* *a bent and twisted witch*

4 A **metaphor** creates a stronger image: the enormous tree, *a bent and twisted witch*, stood black against the sky

5 Add **personification** for extra effect: the enormous tree, *a bent and twisted witch, cackling and crackling, hovered* against the skyline

Try this method yourself on a piece of paper for the following: a car; a building; happiness; eating.

You will need descriptive writing, to some degree, in both your longer and shorter writing tasks.

• You may use it to add interest to your creative writing. For example, you could describe the buildings or the people in the story you wrote earlier (see page 38).

• You may be given a specific descriptive writing task, as in the examples below.

Complete one of the tasks below. Spend about 30 minutes on it.

Answers and guidance are on page 126.

> **HINTS**
> • Ensure that the **type of description** you use suits the **form**, **audience** and **purpose** of your writing. For example, metaphors may not suit a factual piece, but a few really good ones would improve a creative story.
> • Imagery should be used to **create a picture** in the mind of your reader.
> • Go for **quality rather than quantity** – too much description can be as damaging as not enough.

SHORTER WRITING TASK
Describe a train journey you have undertaken, for a brother or sister who was not able to go with you.

You should include a description of:

★ the train itself

★ what you saw on the way

★ your feelings

SHORTER WRITING TASK
Give a description of your school for a 'twin-town' magazine that will be sent to fellow students in Germany.

You should include a description of:

★ the setting of the school, its situation in relation to the rest of the town

★ the buildings and facilities

★ what it is like to be a student in the school

Persuasive writing comes in many different forms: advertisements try to persuade you to buy; speeches try to convince you to see a particular point of view; letters may offer advice. The main purpose of this type of writing is to attempt to change the mind of the audience.

In your Test you may be given a specific task asking you to present a case or give advice. On the other hand, you may be expected to influence your readers in a writing task that is largely to do with explaining or informing.

TASK
Use the examples from the passage below to make a 10-point checklist of the persuasion techniques that you could use when writing a persuasive text yourself.

Answers and guidance are on page 127.

WHAT ARE THE FEATURES OF PERSUASIVE WRITING?

Here is an example of persuasive writing from the back of a cereal packet. It is 'disguised' as a letter to the consumer. Look carefully at the features of persuasive writing – language and structure – that have been used.

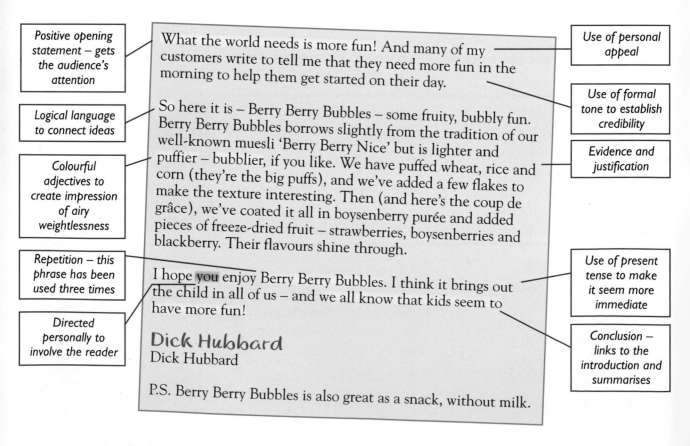

Positive opening statement – gets the audience's attention

Logical language to connect ideas

Colourful adjectives to create impression of airy weightlessness

Repetition – this phrase has been used three times

Directed personally to involve the reader

Use of personal appeal

Use of formal tone to establish credibility

Evidence and justification

Use of present tense to make it seem more immediate

Conclusion – links to the introduction and summarises

What the world needs is more fun! And many of my customers write to tell me that they need more fun in the morning to help them get started on their day.

So here it is – Berry Berry Bubbles – some fruity, bubbly fun. Berry Berry Bubbles borrows slightly from the tradition of our well-known muesli 'Berry Berry Nice' but is lighter and puffier – bubblier, if you like. We have puffed wheat, rice and corn (they're the big puffs), and we've added a few flakes to make the texture interesting. Then (and here's the coup de grâce), we've coated it all in boysenberry purée and added pieces of freeze-dried fruit – strawberries, boysenberries and blackberry. Their flavours shine through.

I hope you enjoy Berry Berry Bubbles. I think it brings out the child in all of us – and we all know that kids seem to have more fun!

Dick Hubbard
Dick Hubbard

P.S. Berry Berry Bubbles is also great as a snack, without milk.

WRITING TASK

Write a supermarket handout to convince customers that they should buy more frozen foods because they are convenient, cheap and high quality.

Whilst features of layout and design may be necessary, no credit will be given for artwork.

You should spend about 30 minutes on this task.

PLANNING

Introduce the case for frozen foods:

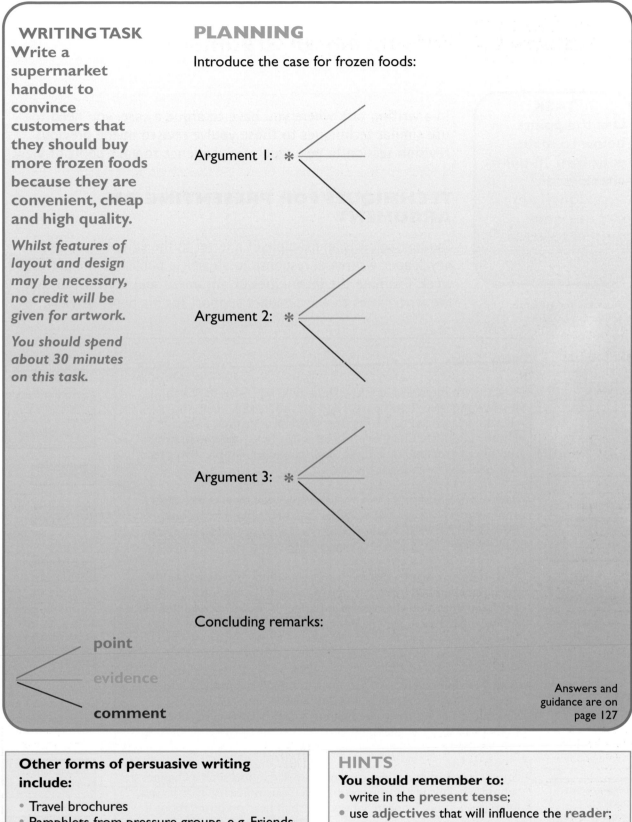

Argument 1: *

Argument 2: *

Argument 3: *

Concluding remarks:

point

evidence

comment

Answers and guidance are on page 127

Other forms of persuasive writing include:

- Travel brochures
- Pamphlets from pressure groups, e.g. Friends of the Earth, League against Cruel Sports
- Book blurbs
- Newspaper or magazine articles
- Junk mail

HINTS

You should remember to:

- write in the **present tense**;
- use **adjectives** that will influence the **reader**;
- apply some persuasive devices such as **rhetorical questions** and **repetition**;
- use **personal pronouns** such as 'you', 'my', 'we'.

TASK
Use the points below to make your own 10-point checklist of techniques you can use when writing to argue a point of view.

Answers and guidance are on page 128.

In a writing task where you have to argue a case, you need to use similar techniques to those you've revised in the previous revision session to persuade your audience to your point of view.

TECHNIQUES FOR PRESENTING AN ARGUMENT

The text below is an example of a letter to the editor of a national newspaper, written in response to an article published the previous week. Examine the techniques of argument and persuasion that the writer uses to win people's support for his point of view.

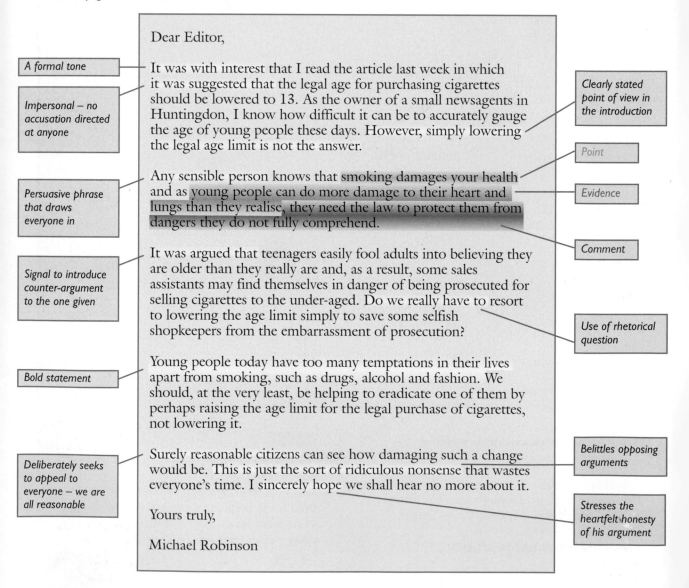

Dear Editor,

It was with interest that I read the article last week in which it was suggested that the legal age for purchasing cigarettes should be lowered to 13. As the owner of a small newsagents in Huntingdon, I know how difficult it can be to accurately gauge the age of young people these days. However, simply lowering the legal age limit is not the answer.

Any sensible person knows that smoking damages your health and as young people can do more damage to their heart and lungs than they realise, they need the law to protect them from dangers they do not fully comprehend.

It was argued that teenagers easily fool adults into believing they are older than they really are and, as a result, some sales assistants may find themselves in danger of being prosecuted for selling cigarettes to the under-aged. Do we really have to resort to lowering the age limit simply to save some selfish shopkeepers from the embarrassment of prosecution?

Young people today have too many temptations in their lives apart from smoking, such as drugs, alcohol and fashion. We should, at the very least, be helping to eradicate one of them by perhaps raising the age limit for the legal purchase of cigarettes, not lowering it.

Surely reasonable citizens can see how damaging such a change would be. This is just the sort of ridiculous nonsense that wastes everyone's time. I sincerely hope we shall hear no more about it.

Yours truly,

Michael Robinson

Annotations:

- A formal tone
- Impersonal – no accusation directed at anyone
- Persuasive phrase that draws everyone in
- Signal to introduce counter-argument to the one given
- Bold statement
- Deliberately seeks to appeal to everyone – we are all reasonable
- Clearly stated point of view in the introduction
- Point
- Evidence
- Comment
- Use of rhetorical question
- Belittles opposing arguments
- Stresses the heartfelt honesty of his argument

SHORTER WRITING TASK

Write a speech **against** the following proposal, to be given at a school council meeting.

You should spend about 30 minutes on this task.

It has been proposed that no students should be allowed to cycle to your school. The arguments for this decision have been given by the Headteacher as:

★ Cycling to school is dangerous and could cause accidents.

★ There is nowhere to store bicycles safely on school property.

★ Students who cycle often fail to complete homework or bring PE kit to school because they say they cannot transport all that is needed on their bikes.

point

evidence

comment

PLANNING

Use this planning sheet to help you to structure what you are going to say.

Introduce the case against the proposed banning of bicycles:

Argument 1: *

Argument 2: *

Argument 3: *

Concluding summary:

Answers and guidance are on page 128.

HINTS

You should remember to:
- Adopt a **formal, impersonal** tone.
- Avoid making comments directed at anyone in particular.
- Give **evidence** to support the points you make.
- **Summarise** your arguments in the conclusion.
- Use **rhetorical questions** if appropriate.

TASK
Use the example below to help you make a 10-point checklist of what you need to do when writing advice.

Answers and guidance are on page 128.

If you undertake a writing task where you are expected to give advice, then you should balance persuasion and argument. You need to be careful of the tone you use and the way in which you introduce your arguments.

TECHNIQUES YOU CAN USE

Here is an example of a text written to advise young people about things they should consider before keeping tropical fish as pets. Look carefully at the techniques that have been used.

Upbeat introduction that will appeal to target audience

Clearly directed at second person (you) making it more personal

Deals with points in a logical or chronological order

Signals the end of the advice

Introduces some humour, which helps keep attention

Thinking of Keeping Tropical Fish?

Read our helpful advice before you buy.

Are you fascinated by the colours, shapes and movement of fish from distant oceans? Keeping tropical fish at home can be an intriguing and rewarding experience. However, there are a few points that you should consider before you take the plunge. Following our advice could save you from a sinking disaster later on.

To begin with, tropical fish aren't cheap. Have you considered how much you have got to spend in order to purchase the fish and the equipment you'd really like? Sometimes your choice is limited by your budget, so do some research first and find out what you can actually afford, before getting carried away by your dreams.

Next, tropical fish need a good deal of space. The cruel little round goldfish bowl of days gone by is a bit out of date in the twenty-first century. Have you thought about where you are going to put your tank? It is a good idea to talk this over with your family before you decide that the dining room table will do nicely. Don't forget that your tank will need to be near an electric socket, to run the lights and water filtering system.

Finally, tropical fish need attention. Their water, for example, needs checking for oxygen levels and temperature, and they also need regular feeding. What is going to happen to your fish when you and the family go away for a holiday? Fish kennels are pretty hard to find. Think about who could look after your pets in your absence before you bring them home.

Problems solved … good luck if you decide to go ahead.

Don't forget to tell your parents, tropical fish are very educational!

Reason why advice should be followed

Makes it sound like something they may have thought of already

Signals an important idea

A gentle reminder rather than an abrupt piece of advice

Makes it sound as if problems can be overcome

SHORTER WRITING TASK

Your eleven-year-old cousin has lived all her life in India but will be returning to England with her family in December to live in your neighbourhood. She has written to ask your advice about how she can best make friends and settle into her new English school.

Write a reply to your cousin, which includes an informal letter layout.

You should spend about 30 minutes on this task.

In your letter you should include general advice about:

★ **overcoming practical difficulties**, such as finding your way around, knowing when and where you can eat;

★ **making friends**, for example by showing an interest in others or not being too nervous;

★ **settling down to work** by staying out of trouble, answering questions in class, doing your homework.

PLANNING

Introduction that includes some brief background information about the school in general:

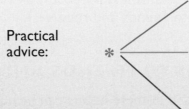

point

evidence

comment

Practical advice: ✳

Advice about making friends: ✳

Advice about studying: ✳

Concluding comments:

Answers and guidance are on page 129.

HINTS
• Use a **friendly, informal tone.**
• **Keep to the point** by focusing on the advice rather than information or gossip.
• If you need guidance on letter layout, see page 60.

Some tasks that are given in your Test may require you to write a letter. You need to make sure that you know the different conventions for writing formal letters (usually written for business purposes) and informal letters (usually written to friends and relatives).

LETTERS TO FRIENDS AND FAMILY

The tone used in these letters can be quite informal – even if you are writing to Great Aunt Agnes to thank her for the birthday gift.

SHORTER WRITING TASK
(The full task was given on page 59. This page will help you to lay out this informal letter correctly.)

Write a reply to your cousin that includes an informal letter layout.

Your address here

The date

Greeting

Paragraphs as outlined in the planning on page 59.

Appropriate ending, e.g. 'With love from'

Signed using the name the person calls you by

Informal letter checklist

✓ Your address on the right-hand side of the page.

✓ The date on the right-hand side of the page.

✓ A greeting such as 'Dear' or 'My dear' but not 'Hi there'.

✓ An ending which is less formal than for a business letter, such as 'With love' or 'Best wishes' (even Great Aunt Agnes deserves more than 'Yours sincerely'!).

FORMAL OR BUSINESS LETTER

Answers
and
guidance
are on
page 129.

This type of letter includes: letters of complaint or asking for advice; applying for a job; writing to a newspaper editor to put your point of view; replying to letters requesting information, etc. The tone of these letters needs to be formal.

SHORTER WRITING TASK

Your grandfather has asked you to write a letter to the council to complain about the poor state of the pavements in his neighbourhood.
The paving slabs are dangerously uneven and piles of litter have not been cleared for weeks.

Write the letter, addressed to the highways department of your local council offices. You may make up an appropriate address.
You should spend about 30 minutes on this task.

Your address
(no name here)

Name and address
of the person you
are writing to

(leave a line between
date and greeting)

Date – day, month (use
the word) and year

Greeting, in this case: 'Dear Sir,'

Paragraph 1 – state clearly why you are writing.
Paragraph 2 – give the details of what you want to say.
Final paragraph – say what you would like to see done
as a result of your letter.

Formal, appropriate ending,
here: 'Yours faithfully,' or
'Yours sincerely,'

Your signature

Your name printed
clearly

Formal/business letter checklist

✓ Your own address first on the right side of the page.

✓ The name of the person you are writing to and/or their job title on the left.

✓ The full address of the person you are writing to on the left.

✓ The date in full on the right.

✓ A conventional greeting against the margin, e.g. 'Dear Sir or Madam'.

✓ A conventional ending against the margin: 'Yours faithfully' (if you have not written to the person before) or 'Yours sincerely' (if you know or have written to the person before).

HINTS

- Don't put your surname at the end of an informal letter, but always put it at the end of a formal one.
- A formal letter ought to have at least three paragraphs.
- The 'Yours' in the ending has a capital letter, but the next word does not.
- The layout conventions when word-processing a letter are different from handwritten versions.

FOCUS ON WRITING

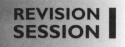

REVISION SESSION I

Analysing plot, language and character

> The Shakespeare scenes and plays that are set for the Test change from year to year. However, the questions will always be similar. The following revision sessions give you help with the techniques you need for answering these questions successfully.

STEPS TO SUCCESS ON THE SHAKESPEARE PAPER

1 Begin by making sure that you fully understand what the question is asking you to do by highlighting and annotating key words, as is shown in this example of a task on *Macbeth*.

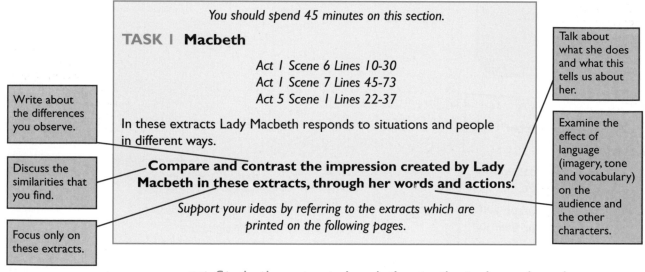

You should spend 45 minutes on this section.

TASK I Macbeth

> Act I Scene 6 Lines 10-30
> Act I Scene 7 Lines 45-73
> Act 5 Scene I Lines 22-37

In these extracts Lady Macbeth responds to situations and people in different ways.

Compare and contrast the impression created by Lady Macbeth in these extracts, through her words and actions.

Support your ideas by referring to the extracts which are printed on the following pages.

Annotations:
- Write about the differences you observe.
- Discuss the similarities that you find.
- Focus only on these extracts.
- Talk about what she does and what this tells us about her.
- Examine the effect of language (imagery, tone and vocabulary) on the audience and the other characters.

2 Study the extracts in relation to the task you have been given. Make annotations and use highlighting to help you pick out useful quotations that could later be used as evidence. To see how this can be done, look at the extracts from *Macbeth* on pages 63 and 64.
- In the first extract opposite the annotations and comments have been made for you.
- In the second extract on page 64 important points have been highlighted for you to comment on.
- The third extract on page 64 has been left blank for you to select quotations and add comments yourself.

3 In order to do well you must have a good overall knowledge of the play, but you must focus your response clearly on the extracts you have been given.

4 Plan your response to the task, making sure you cover all the major points.

5 Use the point, evidence, comment technique to ensure that you clearly relate what you have to say to the extracts you have been given.

EXTRACTS FOR TASK 1: MACBETH

This extract has been annotated for you. **Add any further points that you wish to make.**

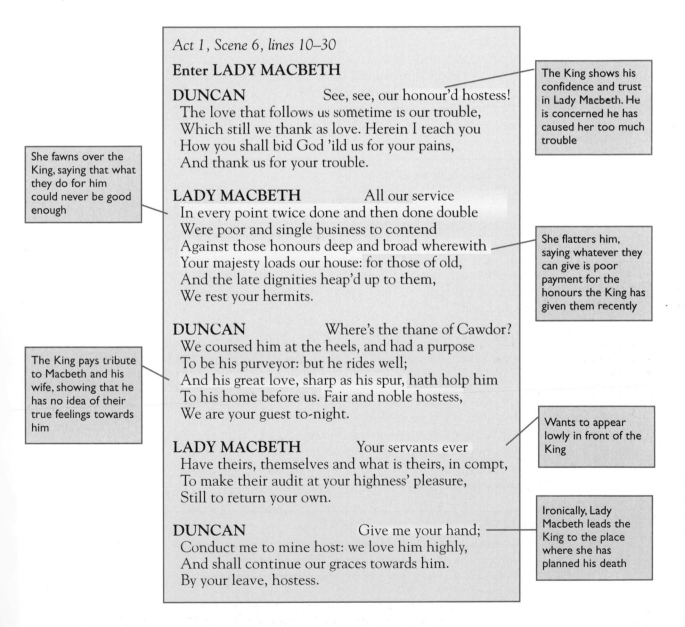

Act 1, Scene 6, lines 10–30

Enter LADY MACBETH

DUNCAN   See, see, our honour'd hostess!
The love that follows us sometime is our trouble,
Which still we thank as love. Herein I teach you
How you shall bid God 'ild us for your pains,
And thank us for your trouble.

> The King shows his confidence and trust in Lady Macbeth. He is concerned he has caused her too much trouble

LADY MACBETH   All our service
In every point twice done and then done double
Were poor and single business to contend
Against those honours deep and broad wherewith
Your majesty loads our house: for those of old,
And the late dignities heap'd up to them,
We rest your hermits.

> She fawns over the King, saying that what they do for him could never be good enough

> She flatters him, saying whatever they can give is poor payment for the honours the King has given them recently

DUNCAN   Where's the thane of Cawdor?
We coursed him at the heels, and had a purpose
To be his purveyor: but he rides well;
And his great love, sharp as his spur, hath holp him
To his home before us. Fair and noble hostess,
We are your guest to-night.

> The King pays tribute to Macbeth and his wife, showing that he has no idea of their true feelings towards him

LADY MACBETH   Your servants ever
Have theirs, themselves and what is theirs, in compt,
To make their audit at your highness' pleasure,
Still to return your own.

> Wants to appear lowly in front of the King

DUNCAN   Give me your hand;
Conduct me to mine host: we love him highly,
And shall continue our graces towards him.
By your leave, hostess.

> Ironically, Lady Macbeth leads the King to the place where she has planned his death

Now it is your turn to annotate the highlighted words and phrases below.

Act 1, Scene 7, lines 45–59

MACBETH   Prithee, peace:
I dare do all that may become a man;
Who dares do more is none.

LADY MACBETH   What beast was't, then,
That made you break this enterprise to me?
When you durst do it, then you were a man;
And, to be more than what you were, you would
Be so much more the man. Nor time nor place
Did then adhere, and yet you would make both:
They have made themselves, and that their fitness now
Does unmake you. I have given suck, and know
How tender 'tis to love the babe that milks me:
I would, while it was smiling in my face,
Have pluck'd my nipple from his boneless gums,
And dash'd the brains out, had I so sworn as you
Have done to this.

Act 5, Scene 1, lines 22–37

Make your own annotations and comments around this extract.

Doctor You see, her eyes are open.

Gentlewoman Ay, but their sense is shut.

Doctor What is it she does now? Look, how she rubs her hands.

Gentlewoman It is an accustomed action with her, to seem thus washing her hands: I have known her continue in this a quarter of an hour.

LADY MACBETH Yet here's a spot.

Doctor Hark! she speaks: I will set down what comes from her, to satisfy my remembrance the more strongly.

LADY MACBETH Out, damned spot! out, I say! – One: two: why, then, 'tis time to do't. – Hell is murky! – Fie, my lord, fie! a soldier, and afeard? What need we fear who knows it, when none can call our power to account? – Yet who would have thought the old man to have had so much blood in him?

HINTS
- Remember to distinguish between Macbeth the character and *Macbeth* the play, by using italics or inverted commas.
- Make sure that you **refer to all the extracts** given in your response.
- **Keep quotations short** and to the point, enclosed within inverted commas.

Answers and guidance are on page 130.

WRITING YOUR RESPONSE

Once you have examined the task and the extracts, you should start to plan your response. As you do so, remember:

- Time is short – select the most important points.
- Relate the task topic clearly to the extracts you have been given.
- Draw your examples, quotations and comment from the given extracts.
- Cover the points indicated in the bullet points beneath the task (they do not have to be in the given order).

Use the outline below as a guide to structuring your response and then continue the points where indicated ...:

Don't forget:

point, evidence, comment

1 Begin by making a **point**:
In the first extract Lady Macbeth demonstrates her dishonesty as she pretends to be a humble hostess to the King...

2 Support this with **evidence**, usually as a quotation or reference to the text:
as is shown when she says, 'Your servants ever'.

3 Follow up with a **comment** which links back to the task topic:
This shows her treacherous character as she is really deceiving the King, to make him feel safe in her hands.

Begin by showing an understanding, acknowledging the task	Lady Macbeth is an interesting central character in 'Macbeth'. At the beginning of the play, the way she uses situations to her advantage and changes her character tells us she ...

Clear statement linked to the task

Looks at her actions	In the first extract Lady Macbeth is shown to be dishonest and insincere through her flattery of the King. For example, when Duncan arrives at the castle she tricks him into believing ...

Point

Evidence

How others respond	From this we can see that other characters find her charming and ...

Comment

Language and effect	On the other hand, we see a different side to Lady Macbeth's character in the second extract, where she is brutal and honest. She insults Macbeth for being weak by saying, 'When you durst do it, then you were a man', which shows that she knows how to manipulate people by taunting them.

Language and effect

In this extract Lady Macbeth's bloodthirsty character is shown through the vivid language she uses, such as 'dash'd the brains out' ...

Conclusion draws points together	However, the third extract, towards the end of the play, shows us that Lady Macbeth is not as strong as we thought. Here her actions, walking and talking in her sleep, show a very different side to her character ...

The three extracts each show a different side to Lady Macbeth's character: the charming but dishonest hostess, the manipulative and brutal wife and the guilt-ridden sleepwalker ...

Answers and guidance are on pages 131–132.

FOCUS ON SHAKESPEARE

Shakespeare's theatre lacked the lighting and other effects that we use today to create a mood; he relied on his words to convey an atmosphere. Tasks on the Shakespeare Paper may ask you to discuss the mood and tone of Shakespeare's language and the effect this creates on the audience.

HOW TO TACKLE THIS SORT OF TASK SUCCESSFULLY

TASK 2 Henry V
In this extract Henry responds to the insulting present of tennis balls from the Dauphin.

How does Shakespeare develop a mood of anger and tension in this extract to maintain the interest of his audience?

Before you begin you should think about:
• the effect of Henry's language;
• how Henry uses imagery;
• the way Henry's words create tension towards the Dauphin;
• the way Henry presents himself to others.
In this extract four different colours have been used to highlight the different ways Shakespeare has used language to create tension. Add your own annotations to those already there.

Act 1, Scene 2, lines 273–297

KING

> But tell the Dauphin **I will keep my state,**
> **Be like a king** and show my sail of greatness
> When I do rouse me in **my throne of France:**
> For that **I have laid by my majesty**
> **And plodded like a man for working-days,**
> But **I will rise there** with so full a glory
> That I will dazzle all the eyes of France,
> Yea, strike the Dauphin blind to look on us.
> And tell the pleasant prince this mock of his
> Hath turn'd his balls to gun-stones; and his soul
> Shall stand sore charged for the wasteful vengeance
> That shall fly with them: for many a thousand widows
> Shall this his mock mock out of their dear husbands;
> Mock mothers from their sons, mock castles down;
> And some are yet ungotten and unborn
> That shall have cause to curse the Dauphin's scorn.
> But this lies all within **the will of God,**
> **To whom I do appeal;** and in whose name
> Tell you the Dauphin I am coming on,
> To venge me as I may and to put forth
> **My rightful hand** in a well-hallow'd cause.
> So get you hence in peace; and tell the Dauphin
> His jest will savour but of shallow wit,
> When thousands weep more than did laugh at it.
> Convey them with safe conduct. Fare you well.
> **Exeunt Ambassadors**

Annotations:

Shows he worked like an ordinary man, which will be useful later

Repetition emphasises his anger, echoing bouncing balls

Metaphor – linked with sailing across the Channel to France

The Dauphin will be blamed, not Henry

Answers and guidance are on pages 132–133.

HOW TO STRUCTURE YOUR ANSWER

In the Test, marks are awarded for your **written expression** as well as your understanding and response to the text. The way in which you structure your answer is therefore important. Once you have identified the key points from the extract, you need to **plan** and **organise** your response.

There are two approaches that you could use:

1 Go through the extract chronologically, discussing the points in relation to the anger and tension as they occur.

2 Group your comments into the elements outlined in the bullet points attached to the question and highlighted in different colours on the page opposite.

Option 1 is the more straightforward, but using this method will make it more difficult for you to achieve a level 7.

Option 2 is a more sophisticated approach. It could help you to achieve higher levels, but using it requires sound understanding and careful organisation before you start to write.

Whichever option you choose, you must begin and end your response in a well-structured way.

Write an introduction which:
• shows that you understand the task/question, without giving a direct answer yet;
• gives a general response to the points the question raises;
• is related to the context of the extract.

> Henry as king is a changed man. Shakespeare uses the insulting gift of the tennis balls from the Dauphin to demonstrate he is ready for a challenge. His angry, tense response in the extract creates interest for the audience through his

Write a conclusion which:
• revisits the focus of the task/question;
• draws together the points that have been made in the essay;
• answers the question – if there is one.

> In this extract Shakespeare uses tension and anger through his clever use of language to create the character of a very regal king. Henry holds the interest of the audience through his controlled and inspired response to the insult. This is important because Henry is a dominant central character in the play that is to follow.

HINTS
• Focus on the **language** of the extract.
• Select your **quotations** and evidence with care.
• **Plan** the structure of your response.

Now write your response to Task 2.

Writing as a character in the play

Empathy tasks, where you are asked to 'step into the shoes' of a character and write from their point of view, are another approach that is used on the Shakespeare Paper. In questions like this, the examiners will still be looking at how well you understand Shakespeare's dramatic skill and use of language, but the focus is slightly different.

If you understand the characters well, an empathy task is a good opportunity to use your creative talents. However, you still need to maintain your focus on the extract, on your awareness of Shakespeare's language and on structuring your response well.

HOW TO TACKLE THIS SORT OF TASK SUCCESSFULLY

HINTS

- In this type of task, you must write in the **first person** (I), as if you are the character concerned.
- Remember that Lady Macbeth is the queen and you would be in fear of her.
- As the doctor you would not know what she was talking about, but you may have suspicions.
- Make sure that you match your **expression and language** to the character, the context of the extract and the task that has been set.
- Introduce **quotations** from the extract in as natural a way as possible, but remember to use inverted commas.

TASK 3 Macbeth

In this scene the Doctor has been called upon by the Gentlewoman to observe Lady Macbeth because she is concerned about her health.

As the Doctor, write a personal and confidential account of what he has observed during his visit.

Before you begin to write

You should think about what the doctor has said and witnessed:
- Why he was called to the castle and his expectations.
- Lady Macbeth's appearance and behaviour.
- His reactions to what he has seen and heard.
- What he should do as a result of his visit.

What you need to do next
- Annotate the question.
- Examine the extract opposite and, using the highlighting and annotating technique, select the key points that you will need to use in your response.
- Plan your response, making sure that you structure and paragraph your work with care.
- Begin with an interesting opening and end with a definite conclusion.

Now write your response to Task 3.

Answers and guidance are on pages 133–134.

LADY MACBETH   The thane of Fife had a wife: where is she now? –
What, will these hands ne'er be clean? – No more o' that, my lord,
no more o' that: you mar all with this starting.

Doctor   Go to, go to; you have known what you should not.

Gentlewoman   She has spoke what she should not,
I am sure of that: heaven knows what she has known.

LADY MACBETH   Here's the smell of the blood still: all the
perfumes of Arabia will not sweeten this little hand. Oh, oh, oh!

Doctor   What a sigh is there! The heart is sorely charged.

Gentlewoman   I would not have such a heart in my bosom for the
dignity of the whole body.

Doctor   Well, well, well, –

Gentlewoman   Pray God it be, sir.

Doctor   This disease is beyond my practice: yet I have known
those which have walked in their sleep who have died
holily in their beds.

LADY MACBETH   Wash your hands, put on your nightgown;
look not so pale. – I tell you yet again, Banquo's buried; he
cannot come out on's grave.

Doctor   Even so?

LADY MACBETH   To bed, to bed! there's knocking at the gate:
come, come, come, come, give me your hand. What's
done cannot be undone. – To bed, to bed, to bed!   **Exit**

Doctor   Will she go now to bed?

Gentlewoman   Directly.

Doctor   Foul whisperings are abroad: unnatural deeds
Do breed unnatural troubles: infected minds
To their deaf pillows will discharge their secrets:
More needs she the divine than the physician.
God, God forgive us all! Look after her;
Remove from her the means of all annoyance,
And still keep eyes upon her. So, good night:
My mind she has mated, and amazed my sight.
I think, but dare not speak.

Writing as a director

While studying Shakespeare's words, we must never forget that the plays were written to be performed. Some tasks in the Shakespeare test focus specifically on this crucial point, asking candidates to put themselves in the director's chair.

HOW TO TACKLE THIS SORT OF TASK SUCCESSFULLY

- Have an overall idea of the effect you wish to create through the words and actions of the given extract.
- Be aware that the audience will react to the body language and facial expressions of the actors.
- Understand that words can be said in different ways to create different effects.

TASK 4
Much Ado About Nothing

In this extract from *Much Ado About Nothing*, Beatrice gives Benedick a challenge.

You have been asked to direct this part of the scene to help the other students in your class gain a better understanding of the two characters and their situation.

Write an explanation to the two actors playing the parts of Beatrice and Benedick, outlining the effect you want to create and how it could be achieved.

Answers and guidance are on pages 134–135.

Act IV, Scene 1, lines 288–313

BEATRICE You have stayed with me a happy hour: I was about to protest I loved you.

BENEDICK And do it with all thy heart.

BEATRICE I love you with so much of my heart that none is left to protest.

BENEDICK Come, bid me do anything for thee.

BEATRICE Kill Claudio.

BENEDICK Ha! Not for the wide world.

BEATRICE You kill me to deny it. Farewell.

BENEDICK Tarry, sweet Beatrice.

BEATRICE I am gone, though I am here: there is no love in you: nay, I pray you, let me go.

BENEDICK Beatrice

BEATRICE In faith, I will go.

BENEDICK We'll be friends first.

BEATRICE You dare easier be friends with me than fight with mine enemy.

BENEDICK Is Claudio thine enemy?

BEATRICE Is he not approved in the height of a villain, that has slandered, scorned, dishonoured my kinswoman? O! that I were a man. What! Bear her in hand until they come to take hands, and then, with public accusation, uncover slander, unmitigated rancour, – O God, that I were a man! I would eat his heart in the market-place.

WHAT YOU NEED TO DO

As you would with other types of questions, begin by:
1 annotating and highlighting the key words in the task;
2 annotating and adding a commentary on the extract you have been given.

Next make notes in response to these questions:

Context and character
- What has been happening just before this episode?
- Who are these two people and what are they like?
- How do they behave towards each other?
- Do their words have any hidden messages that the audience will understand, even though the characters might not (dramatic irony)?

Delivery and expression
- What general tone do the characters use? (e.g. Do they sound angry, impatient, serious, etc?)
- How will you bring out significant points so the audience knows they are important? (Do they speak quietly or shout at each other?)

Body language
- How should the characters look at each other whilst they are speaking? (e.g. should they make eye contact or look in another direction?)
- How do they move their bodies? (How do they use their hands when they speak? Do they show they are angry by pacing the floor?)

Action and effect
- What does Shakespeare want the audience to understand about these two characters from the way they speak and act towards each other?
- How do they move in response to each other as the scene progresses?
- What will the audience see and understand from your directions?

STRUCTURING YOUR RESPONSE

There are two ways in which you can answer a question like this.

Option 1: A character-based response

1 Briefly introduce the context of the scene, giving some background of plot and character.
2 Explain the overall effect, tone and mood you wish to create between the two characters.
3 Give examples of how Beatrice should speak and act.
4 Give examples of how Benedick should speak and act.
5 Conclude by explaining how you think these effects will help the audience to better understand the characters and their situation.

Option 2: A topic-based response

This would use the headings given in the research and planning above as a guide for developing and organising your paragraphs.

> ### HINTS
> - It is just as important in this type of task to **give quotations**.
> - Use the **point, evidence, comment** technique to support your explanation.
> - Show clearly that you **understand the language** of the extract.
> - Consider the possibility of **irony** – meaning may be conveyed beneath the surface of the words.

Now write your response to Task 4.

TEST PRACTICE

How to tackle the Reading Paper

What the Test will be like

- At the beginning of the Reading Paper you will be given **15 minutes** to read a booklet containing three extracts. One will be fiction and two will be non-fiction, such as autobiography, travel writing, newspaper and magazine articles.

- After this time you will be told to open the Answer booklet containing the questions related to the extracts. You will then be given **1 hour** to write your responses.

- There will be **several questions for each extract**. Each question will have a particular focus, such as asking you to deduce information by reading between the lines, or commenting on the writer's language (see revision sessions 1–5 on pages 2–21).

- Some questions will require only very short answers, others will need longer ones. The **number of marks** awarded will vary from question to question and will act as a guide as to how much you need to write.

Before the Test

- Use the earlier **revision sessions** in this book to remind you of the types of questions that may be set and the best strategies for answering them.

- Increase your own awareness of different types of writing by reading **a wide variety of texts**, for example information leaflets, quality newspapers and magazines, even advertisements.

- **Improve your vocabulary and awareness of language** by looking up words in a dictionary, or thinking about why a particular word has been chosen and the effect it creates.

In the 15-minute reading time

- Use your time effectively by reading each extract slowly and carefully **at least once**.

- For each extract think about:
  - **the form** – what kind of writing is it?
  - **the purpose** – why has it been written?
  - **the reader** – who has it been written for?

- Make a note of the **tone**, **language** and **expression** that each writer has used.

During the Test

- Take time to read the questions for each extract very carefully.

- Once you know the questions, **re-read or scan the extract**, annotating particular points and features by using highlighters or coloured pens.

- **Use the mark and space given for each question to guide your response.** For example, a question that is worth 2 marks probably requires you to make two brief points, whereas one worth 5 marks followed by several lines for writing needs a fuller, more detailed, response.

- **Be concise**, don't waffle.

- **Use the point – evidence – comment formula** where appropriate.

- If you don't know, **guess** – you won't lose marks for trying, but if you don't try you won't get anything!

At the end of the Test

- Leave enough time to read through and **check your answers**.

Journey to Morocco

Contents

On the following pages you will find three reading texts:

Morocco has been a place of fascination for people from all over the world for centuries. Its colourful markets and delicious food still attract many visitors seeking something different and enchanting.

If you were to visit this remarkable place, what would capture your interest?

Remember

- You have 15 minutes to read these texts.

- During this time you must not write or open the Answer booklet.

- At the end of 15 minutes you will have 1 hour to answer the questions.

Hideous Kinky: an extract from the novel by Esther Freud

Hideous Kinky is an autobiographical novel based on the childhood experiences in Morocco of the author, Esther Freud, during the 1960s. In this extract she describes the food and entertainment that the sisters share with their mother and their new friends in the city of Marrakech. The story is told by the younger of the two sisters.

Mum collected her letters from the Post Office and the money that had arrived at the bank, and we all went to eat at our old café in the Djemaa El Fna. The waiter, the cook and the manager all welcomed us as if we had been away for ever, and we took a table right on the edge of the square, half in and half out of the shade.

5 Mum was wearing her Biba dress and her eyes sparkled. 'Whatever you want for lunch,' she announced.

'Fanta please,' I sang every time the waiter passed. 'Fanta please.'

We ate Moroccan salad and a plate of chicken <u>tajine</u> that was almost the size of the table and arrived with its flowerpot hat on.

10 As we ate Mum looked through her letters. 'My mother is praying that we'll all be home safe and sound for Christmas,' she read. 'And she hopes the children are looking after their teeth.' She frowned. Our one tube of toothpaste had run out in the first few weeks of

15 spring in the Mellah.

My Fanta gurgled through its straw.

Mum folded up the letter and slipped it into its envelope. 'And that's enough Fanta for one day,' she said.

'Now Mob isn't so heavy, can I carry her on my back?' Bea asked

20 quickly, gulping down the remainder of her bottle before any more serious ban could be declared.

Linda shook out her shawl and strapped Mob on, tight across Bea's back. 'Don't go too far,' she shouted after us as we slipped off into the crowd to find Khadija and the beggar girls who roamed the square.

25 We stopped to watch the <u>Gnaoua</u> as they danced like Russians to their brass crackers and drums. Mob stared transfixed over Bea's shoulder as the men squatted and kicked out their legs.

'It's the Fool,' Bea whispered, pointing to a dirty and dishevelled man dancing wildly on the fringes of the group. 'I've seen him before.'

30 As we watched, the Fool took a particularly abandoned leap, tripped, and landed on his back, ripping his threadbare <u>djellaba</u>. The crowd tittered. The Fool picked himself up and, with a moment to fasten his cloak, worked himself back into the dance.

When the music stopped, the Gnaoua offered him a drink. He

35 grinned, dribbling at his new friends, and tried to clasp them in his arms. They smiled down on him, tall and gentle and shimmering blue-black against his dusty face.

The drummer girls called to us as we passed. 'Waa, waa.' They leapt up from their display of painted drums and surrounded us, flapping

40 like butterflies in their brightly coloured caftans. They unstrapped Mob and carried her off to crawl among their rows of drums while they tapped out tunes for her on the tight skin tops. The drummer girls had lengths of braid plaited into their oiled hair and mostly their earrings were a loop of plastic wire hung with beads. They pressed the

45 drums we admired into our hands and before we had a chance to

Glossary
tajine – *a Moroccan dish, like a stew*
Gnaoua – *African dancers*
djellaba – *a loose cloak worn in Morocco*

refuse. One of the girls helped to restrap Mob on to Bea's back. I
caught Bea's eye as we moved away.

'They are forever giving the children things,' Mum had despaired to
Linda, 'and they must be so poor.'

'Poorer than Khadija's mother?' I had asked.   50

But she had gone on mumbling. 'Nothing, they have nothing, and
they give the drums away ...'
As if she could unravel the mystery with words.

Clutching our drums we passed among the stalls of fruit. Water
melons, oranges, prickly pears that were too dangerous to eat. We   55
passed the women at the mouth of the market who sat like sentries in
their high boxes with bread for sale. Some sold round white loaves,
and others black. An old lady squatted by a pile of six oranges and
while we watched she sold one, taking the coins and stowing them
carefully away inside her djellaba, before settling back to wait   60
patiently by her five remaining oranges for the next customer to pass.

'What do you think happens if nothing gets sold?' I asked Bea as we
passed a man dozing in front of a box of peppers.

'They just eat them,' she said.

Khadija, Zara and Saida were engrossed in tormenting a tourist.   65
'Tourist, tourist,' they chanted.

We watched as a man bought a cup of water from the waterman and
a woman in a blue dress stood back to take a photograph. 'Tourist,
tourist.' They held out their hands.

'Tourist,' I muttered under my breath, but my newly washed trousers   70
with Bilal's patch blazing on the knee stopped me from joining in.

'Waa Khadija.' We called them. 'Waa Saida, Waa waa Zara.' And
they ran over to us, leaving the couple to wander unchaperoned back
to their hotel. We squatted in a circle to exchange news. Mob stared
into the black eyes of Khadija's baby sister as her head bobbed against 75
Bea's shoulder. Saida inspected Bilal's patch. Saida was smaller than
me and thin with big black eyes and straight shiny hair. She began to
pick at the patch with her fingers and then when it wouldn't come
loose she held out her hand for it. I looked at her, my mouth dry, and
shook my head so violently she pulled away.   80

That evening as I sat on Bilal's knee begging a scrape of <u>majoun</u>, I
asked, 'Can I keep my trousers and just wear them when we live in
England?'

'If they still fit you,' Bea said.

'Yes, of course,' Mum agreed and ordered another pot of mint tea.

Glossary
majoun – *pudding of dried fruits, nuts and spices*

Holidays in the Muslim world: *Medina at Fez*

Tourists may be scarce, but north Africa is still the wild, kaleidoscopic, beautiful maelstrom it always was. Andrew Gilchrist gets happily lost.

WE ARE IN THE BACK of a battered old silver Merc taxi, a bouncy castle on wheels. Over dunes, ditches, shrubs, rocks and landslides we pound, thinking no beach can
5 be worth this limb-dislocating journey. Then the driver swings left and there it is below: Paradise Beach – about two miles of flat, golden sand glimmering in the midday sun, lapped by big noisy waves and enclosed at
10 either end by mighty cliffs.

Where the road runs out, bony donkeys are hauling cartloads of food, drink and pale western sunworshippers down to the ragbag collection of makeshift cafés along the edge
15 of the near-deserted sands. Out towards the horizon, little boats are nodding inshore to provide freshly-caught sardines for the lunchtime tajines – delicious traditional Moroccan stews spiced up with anything
20 from almonds to olives, pickled lemon rind to prunes. The sardine tajine cost little more than £7. It could have easily fed four.

Paradise Beach lies on the edge of Asilah, a lovely, bite-sized Moroccan town
25 about 45 minutes by taxi or train down the coast from Tangier. With its brightly-painted old quarters, its ramparts straddling the rocks, its palm trees swaying in the coastal breeze and its not-too-pushy market traders,
30 Asilah is the perfect place to ease yourself into Morocco.

And it is worth trying to ease yourself into this country, for big-town Morocco can be a big-time culture shock. There's the
35 hassle in the streets, the haggling in the bazaars, the maelstrom of the medinas, the hustlers, and conmen, and the beggars young, old, desperate and dying. Then there's the money, the taxis, the drinking
40 laws, the food, the heat – and the pitiful attempts to get by on what little French you can remember from school.

Fez was a half-day on the train from Asilah and a first-class ticket cost 30
45 dirhams (£1.80) extra, so it seemed churlish not to. Once the hub of Moroccan trade, culture, religious life and politics, Fez is today chiefly of interest for its gigantic, sprawling medina – a kaleidoscopic maze
50 boasting several outstanding mosques swaddled by about one million narrow, winding, hilly lanes crammed with men, women, children, cats, dogs, donkeys and shops selling everything from traditional
55 Arab clothing to ceramics and, of course, carpets of every size, shape, pattern and form. There are four entrance gates, and whichever one you choose will lead you, as a westerner, into a storm of attention from
60 young boys wanting to be your guide. Rather than trying to get rid of them, which is exhausting and virtually impossible, you might let one tag along with you and kid on he's taking you places, then bung him 10
65 dirhams (60p – a fortune to a young boy) afterwards. If nothing else, it will keep other guides at bay and once you're done, he can show you the way out.

It's no great worry getting lost though. In
70 fact, that's half the fun. Wander in and just get caught up in the dusty, jostling, deafening flow, meandering from stall to shop to café greeted by a regular chorus of: 'Yes please, where you from?'

75 Another half-day in a first-class compartment took us to Marrakech, where we dropped our bags at Hotel Ali, a mecca for backpackers in the medina, and signed up for one of its three-day trips (£57 a head
80 including accommodation and evening meals) that took us up over the wild Atlas

mountains, through some stunning gorges and on to a camel trip across the Sahara. As the sun set behind us, Berber tribesmen led our camels on a two-hour trek towards our tents, where mint tea and a fabulous cous-cous stew awaited. Only half the party slept in the tents, the rest choosing to lie back and gaze at the stars and comet tails, listening to the camels regurgitating what sounded like entire fields of shrubs.

Back in Marrakech, it was time to hit the legendary Djemaa El Fna, the manic square where Morocco in all its madness comes at you like a lorry. There are boys boxing, monkeys dancing, bands busking, men charming cobras, story-tellers ranting, and, among all this, are foodstalls, herb doctors and, inevitably, henna tattooists in case you want to look like a human doodle. If it all gets too much, there are rooftop cafés around the square.

Less than two hours away by bus, the 18th-century coastal town of Essaouira has wood workshops the way some houses have mice. Everywhere you look, there are crates with American addresses written on the side containing tables, chairs and ornaments so magnificently ornate that any self-respecting tree would be happy to have been turned into them.

Just off the main square are the fish souks, about 20 bright white stalls with shade and seating, offering the morning's catch barbecued before your eyes. Ten pounds bought us salad and prawns, followed by sea bass, turbot, crab, sardines and anchovies. Then the main course arrived: lobster. Delicious – and we were probably overcharged.

Moroccan salads come drizzled with argan oil, a remarkable, nutty-tasting foodstuff unique to the country. The delicious dark amber fluid is extracted from the yellow seeds that fall off the argan tree (it is too thorny for humans to pick). But, someone told us, there is another way. Goats have a craving for the seed though their stomachs can't crack its hard casing if swallowed uncrunched. So Moroccans recover the seeds from goats' droppings.

Not the sort of thing you put on the side of the bottle.

The Guardian,
Saturday November 10, 2001

Glossary
souk — *open-air marketplace*

The Country

The Atlantic to the west, the Mediterranean to the north, wonderful beaches, four mountain ranges with cascading waterfalls, century-old cedar forests, eternal snows, immense plains flowering with orange and almond blossom, rivers that lay out a carpet of greenery to the threshold of the desert and carve out the most spectacular gorges: From the Straits of Gibraltar to Mauritania, nature has made Morocco one of the most beautiful countries in the world, the country that is a feast for all the senses.

5

10

Morocco has been inhabited since very early prehistoric times, as the many prehistoric remains show. Then came the Phoenicians, Carthaginians, Berbers, Byzantines, Romans and Vandals before the Arab invasion which took place in the 8th century.

15

20

The Food

Moroccan cuisine offers refined preparations of sun-drenched fruit and vegetables, rare and aromatic spices, delicate fish and succulent meats. This is the very best of Oriental cuisine, famous throughout the world – a real delight for your taste buds. Here are the main Moroccan dishes which you must try.

25

KEBABS: You will see delicious kebabs being cooked in front of you at the entrance to the souk, in squares or at the roadside. A convenient and cheap delight.

30

COUSCOUS: The traditional family dish for Friday lunch, but you will find it every day in restaurants. You can taste many different types of couscous during your visit, for they vary according to the region and the cook's imagination. Try not using cutlery but eating it with your fingers in Moroccan style.

35

40

DISHES FOR RAMADAN: At sunset, the fast (f'tour) is broken with the rich and savoury harira, a soup of meat, lentils and chick peas, with beghrir, little honeycombed pancakes served with melted butter and honey, and with shebbakia, cakes turned in oil then covered in honey. This 'light snack' will tide you over until the real dinner, which is served later in the night.

45

TAJINE: This word designates both the decorated earthenware plate with its distinctive conical cover and the dish itself (meat, chicken or fish stew with vegetables). Taste it and you will understand why tajine is the Moroccan national dish.

50

55

MINT TEA: Refreshing, warming and stimulating, drunk in the morning, after meals or at any time. A pleasure you should never refuse.

Way of Life

60

A respect of local customs is a fundamental act of courtesy in a welcoming country. To avoid embarrassing situations and misunderstandings, comply with common practice.

65

Here are a few essential rules to follow:

- ✔ In Morocco, access to mosques and holy places is forbidden to non-Muslims.
- ✔ Avoid provocative clothing.
- ✔ Accept mint tea when offered, a sign of 70 hospitality.
- ✔ If you are invited to share in a family meal, you should symbolically use the <u>ewer</u> to wash your hands. The meal begins after the master of the house has said the 75 'bismillah' in praise of God. Use your right hand to eat, taste everything, but don't think you have to finish everything in your plate, which is usually impossible!
- ✔ Avoid drinking, eating and smoking in 80 public in daytime during the period of Ramadan.
- ✔ If you want to photograph somebody, don't forget to ask for permission.

Glossary

ewer – *large jug*
muezzin – *mosque official who calls the faithful to prayer*
minaret – *a slender tower of a mosque*

Religion

85

Islam is the official religion in Morocco, but it exists in perfect co-existence with the other religions (freedom to practise other religions of revelation is guaranteed by the constitution).

90

The day is marked by five calls to prayer. The <u>muezzin</u> announces them from the top of his <u>minaret</u>.

During the month of Ramadan, the Moroccans fast, refraining from eating and 95 smoking from sunrise to sunset. Obviously this disturbs daily life. Most Civil Service and public offices, monuments and shops alter their opening hours. However, non-Muslims will always find something to eat in 100 certain restaurants, particularly in hotels. The days may seem long, but the nights are wonderful!

Folklore

Traditions and folk art remain very much alive in Morocco. Music is present everywhere in the country, accompanying festivities and ceremonies. In the towns it has developed into an instrumental form. This is traditional classical or popular Arab music. In rural or Berber tribes, music is intimately linked with poetry and dance. The folk dances are magnificent and accompany the tribes' everyday life. These are the most important ones:

THE ANOUACH in the valleys of the High Atlas: The women form a circle around men playing tambourines.

THE GUEDRA from southern Morocco: The dancer is on her knees, totally covered by a black veil. A throbbing rhythm builds as the dancer's fingers weave and transfix the audience, which goes into a trance.

THE TISSINT DE TATA (from south of Agadir): Women and men dressed in indigo perform the dance of the dagger.

THE GNAOUAS is of African origin: Against an obsessive rhythm, the dancers rival each other with acrobatic feats.

THE TASKIOUINE from the High Atlas close to Ouarzazate: A dance of warriors, powerful and virile. Dressed in white tunics, a powder flask on their shoulders, the dancers beat out the rhythm with their feet and clap their hands energetically.

105

110

115

120

125

130

135

Journey to Morocco

Please read this page, but do not open the booklet until your teacher tells you to start.

First name _____

Last name _____

School _____

Date _____

Write your answers in this booklet.

You may ask for more paper if you need it.

- The paper is 1 hour and 15 minutes long.

- You have 15 minutes to read the Reading booklet before answering the questions in your answer booklet. During this time you should not open your answer booklet.

- You then have 1 hour to write your answers.

- There are 14 questions totalling 32 marks on this paper.

Journey to Morocco

Questions 1–7 are about *Hideous Kinky* (pages 74–75).

1   Underline two words from the list below which you think best describe the mother's attitude towards her daughters:

anxious   thoughtful   easy-going   unsympathetic

generous   insensitive   strict   caring   *(1 mark)*

2   Give a quotation from the section beginning 'Mum collected her letters' (line 1) to 'could be declared' (line 21) which shows that the narrator is a young child.   *(1 mark)*

_____

_____

_____

_____

3   The author says that the Gnaoua 'danced like Russians' (line 25). Find another simile that the author has used and comment on the image it creates.   *(2 marks)*

_____

_____

_____

_____

_____

4   'The Fool picked himself up and, with a moment to fasten his cloak, worked himself back into the dance' (lines 32–33).

What is the purpose of the commas in this sentence?   *(1 mark)*

_____

_____

_____

_____

5 'They are forever giving the children things,' says the children's mother in line 48.

Give two examples (from the paragraph beginning on line 38) that demonstrate the kindness and generosity of the drummer girls. *(2 marks)*

_____

_____

_____

_____

_____

6 '"Tourist," I muttered under my breath, but my newly washed trousers with Bilal's patch blazing on the knee stopped me from joining in' (lines 70–71).

Later in the passage the narrator asks if her trousers could be put away until she returns to England. Explain why you think she makes this request. *(2 marks)*

_____

_____

_____

_____

_____

7 Using an example from the passage as a whole, explain how the author indicates that Bea is the older sister. *(1 mark)*

_____

_____

_____

_____

_____

_____

Questions 8–11 are about *Medina at Fez* (pages 76–77).

8 Explain the purpose of the opening sentence and give two reasons why
you think it is effective.

(3 marks)

_____

_____

_____

_____

9 Here are five sub-headings which
could be used for different
sections of the text.

Number each sub-heading 1–5
to show the order in which they
occur in the text. Number 2 has been done for you.

A	From clothing to ceramics	2
B	A night with the camels	
C	A feast of fish	
D	Rough ride to paradise	
E	Madness in Marrakech	

(2 marks)

10 In paragraph 5, beginning 'Fez was a half-day on the train' (line 43), what
impression does the writer convey of the medina at Fez through his use of
figurative language?

Complete the following table by adding one more metaphor from
paragraph 5 and explain how the choice of language in each case creates
a picture of the medina at Fez.

(3 marks)

Quotation/metaphor	The image that this metaphor creates for the reader
'kaleidoscopic maze'	
'swaddled by about one million narrow, winding, hilly lanes'	

11 Focusing only on the last section of the passage from line 75 onwards, beginning 'Another half-day in a first-class compartment', comment on how the writer conveys his thoughts and experiences to the reader. *(5 marks)*

_____

_____

_____

_____

_____

_____

_____

_____

_____

_____

_____

_____

_____

Questions 12–14 are about *The Pocket Guide* (pages 78–80.

12 How does the writer use punctuation to clarify meaning?
Complete the following table.

(3 marks)

Punctuation feature	Example	How it helps the reader
dash	– a real delight for your taste buds. line 27	
inverted commas	'light snack' line 47	
brackets	(meat, chicken, or fish stew with vegetables) line 53	

13 Are the following statements from the guide fact or opinion? Complete the grid below. Statement A has been done for you.

(1 mark)

	Statement	Fact or opinion
A	'a country that is a feast for all the senses'	Opinion
B	'This is the very best of Oriental cuisine'	
C	'The day is marked by five calls to prayer'	
E	'The folk dances are magnificent'	

14 The purpose of this guide is to give travellers to Morocco information and advice about the country. Explain how the writer demonstrates an awareness of the reader's needs.

You should comment on:

- the writer's use of language

- the structure and organisation of the information

- the ways in which it has been made accessible.   *(5 marks)*

_____

_____

_____

_____

_____

_____

_____

_____

_____

_____

_____

_____

_____

_____

_____

_____

_____

How to tackle the Writing Paper

What is in the Paper

The Writing Paper is 1 hour and 30 minutes long. It gives you an opportunity to demonstrate your writing skills by completing two different tasks. You are advised to spend one hour on Section A, the longer writing task, and 30 minutes on Section B, the shorter writing task. These guidelines include time for planning and checking. It is a important to follow the suggested time limits.

Before the Test

- Revise the work you have done, covering the techniques and approaches used for writing for different purposes. These include: to persuade, to inform, to explain, to review, to argue and to advise.

- Familiarise yourself with the conventions of various different forms of writing such as writing a speech, a leaflet or a letter. Know what is expected.

- Revise spelling of common words that cause you trouble.

When you begin

- Read the instructions for each task very carefully. Make sure that you fully understand what it is you are being asked to do, in particular the intended reader, purpose and form of the task.

- Use the planning page given for Section A before you start. It will help to guide your writing.

- Make your own plan for Section B – a planning page for the shorter writing task isn't given to you.

During the Test

- Begin in a way that immediately catches the attention of the reader. Don't waste time on long introductions – get to the point quickly.

- Make sure that the style and tone of your writing are appropriate to the task.

- Use as wide a vocabulary as you can. Remember it is better to use an incorrectly spelt interesting word than a correctly spelt dull one.

- Spell common words correctly – careless spelling of ordinary words could be costly.

- Vary your sentence structure to engage the interest of your reader and to create different effects.

- Ensure that you organise your paragraphs and use link sentences to move from one topic to another.

- Your handwriting should be clear. Don't worry if you have to cross things out, but do so neatly and make the change obvious.

- Time yourself so you complete your writing before the time is up

In the last FIVE minutes

- Stop writing, start checking, even if you haven't quite finished. You will be amazed how many errors you can spot! Look out for: words left out; confused tenses; spelling errors; overused words; dull words that could be replaced with interesting ones; missing punctuation. Putting them right will gain you more credit than that missing last sentence or two.

Key Stage 3 English National Curriculum

Levels 4–7

Writing Paper

Please read this page, but do not open the booklet until your teacher tells you to start.

Write your name and the name of the school in the space below.

First name: _____

Last name: _____

School: _____

Date: _____

- The paper is 1 hour 30 minutes long, including up to 15 minutes recommended planning time for Section A.

- There are two sections. You are advised to spend:
  1 hour on Section A
  30 minutes on Section B.

- To help you there is a planning page is provided for the task in Section A. This page will not be marked.

- Write your answers in the Writing Paper answer booklet.

Section A: Longer writing task

You should spend about 1 hour on this section

Set Apart?

Write a story about someone who is different, 'set apart' in some way from others in the community.

Imagine what it might feel like to be part of a community and yet know that you are in some way different. It could be: the accent you speak with; a physical difference, such as wearing glasses or being in a wheelchair; being of a different race or culture; being blind or deaf. Such differences can be a strength, but perhaps also a threat to the person or the community in which they live.

The story you tell can be set in any time or place. It can be written from any point of view.

Whatever you choose to write about, you should:

- explore feelings and experiences
- explain the context and setting
- include a crisis and resolution.

(30 marks)

Planning

Before you write, plan the main points of your story.

Setting:

Central character outline of personality:

Experiences:

Exploring feelings:

Crisis:

Resolution:

Section B: Shorter writing task

You should spend about 30 minutes on this section.

Don't believe in fortune tellers

Your 15-year-old cousin has visited a fortune teller and has been told that in the future he/she will marry someone rich and famous. He/she has therefore decided that there is no point devoting any time to schoolwork or exams. You are concerned that your cousin is taking a ridiculous risk by trusting predictions and throwing away the opportunity to make the most of his/her ability.

Your task is to write a letter to your cousin persuading him/her not to trust what the fortune teller has said. You should:

- argue against the dangers of believing in fortune tellers
- offer advice about taking control of his/her life
- persuade him/her to continue with work at school

You should set your letter out in the conventional way.

(20 marks including 4 marks for spelling)

Reading Paper Answers and Guidance

When you have completed the Reading Paper on pages 74–80, preferably to time under test conditions, it is time to see how well you have done. Use this section to mark your answers.

Each question has a focus similar to those explained earlier in the 'Focus on Reading' section pages 2–21. Once you have marked your Test, if you find that you still have a weakness in a particular area, go back and revise that section again.

Questions 1–7 are about *Hideous Kinky* (pages 74–75).

> **1** Underline two words from the list below which you think best describe the mother's attitude towards her daughters.

The words are: <u>easy-going</u> and <u>generous</u>

Explanation: The mother generously orders 'whatever you want for lunch'; later she lets her daughters wander over to the dancers and play with the children, showing she is easy-going. She has also not worried too much about whether they have brushed their teeth. None of the other words accurately describes her attitude.

QUESTION FOCUS:
Deduce, infer, or interpret information, ideas or events.
(1 mark if both words are correctly identified – total 1)

> **2** Give a quotation from the section beginning 'Mum collected the letters' (line 1) to 'could be declared' (line 21) which shows that the narrator is a young child.

Any one of the following:
- '"Fanta please," I sang every time the waiter passed.'
- 'arrived with its flowerpot hat on.'
- 'My Fanta gurgled through its straw.'

QUESTION FOCUS:
Understand, describe, select or retrieve information, ideas or events and use quotations.

(1 mark for giving one correct quotation – total 1)

> **3** The author says that the Gnaoua 'danced like Russians' (line 25). Find another simile that the author has used and comment on the image it creates.

One of the following:
- 'flapping like butterflies in brightly coloured caftans' (lines 39–40). This simile highlights the colourful clothes of the drummer girls, as well as the lightness and swiftness of their movement, which makes them seem like butterflies.
- 'who sat like sentries' (line 56). The simile makes it seem as if the women are guards at the gates of the market, protecting their bread and the market itself.

QUESTION FOCUS:
Explain and comment on the writer's use of language and literary features.

(1 mark for giving a correct simile, 1 mark for explaining the effect it creates – total 2)

QUESTION FOCUS:
Identify and comment
on structure,
organisation of texts
including grammatical
features.
(1 mark)

4 'The Fool picked himself up and, with a moment to fasten his cloak, worked himself back into the dance' (lines 32–33).
What is the purpose of the commas in this sentence?

'The pair of commas in the sentence are being used to mark off a phrase that is giving the reader extra information. They are acting like brackets.

QUESTION FOCUS:
Understand, describe,
select or retrieve
information, ideas or
events and use
quotations.

5 'They are forever giving the children things,' says the children's mother in line 48.
Give two examples that demonstrate the kindness and generosity of the drummer girls.

Any two of the following points:
• The girls took the baby from Bea and let her crawl amongst their drums.
• They tried to amuse the baby by playing tunes on the drums for her.
• They gave Bea and her sister the drums they had admired.
• One of the girls helped to re-strap the baby onto Bea's back.

QUESTION FOCUS:
Deduce, infer, or
interpret information,
ideas or events.

6 '"Tourist," I muttered under my breath, but my newly washed trousers with Bilal's patch blazing on the knee stopped me from joining in' (lines 70–71).
Later in the passage the narrator asks if her trousers could be put away until she returns to England. Explain why you think she makes this request.

Any two of the following points:
• The trousers make her different from the way the other girls are dressed.
• They prevent her from joining in the 'tourist' game because they show she is not a beggar.
• The patch on the trousers had been sewn on by Bilal, which makes it special to her, because she is fond of him.
• Because the patch is special, she doesn't want someone to take the patch, as the girl had tried to do earlier.

(1 mark for any of the
reasons given to a
maximum of 2 – total 2)

QUESTION FOCUS:
Deduce, infer, or
interpret information,
ideas or events.

7 Using an example from the passage as a whole, explain how the author indicates that Bea is the older sister.

Any two of the following points:
• Bea drinks down her Fanta quickly before her mother thinks about her ruining her teeth.
• Bea asks for, and is given, the baby to carry.
• Bea recognises the Fool she has seen before.
• Bea is so wise about what happens to the food that is unsold.
• Bea makes the comment about her sister outgrowing her trousers.

Questions 8–11 are about *Medina at Fez* (pages 76–77).

---

8 Explain the purpose of the opening sentence and comment on its effectiveness.

QUESTION FOCUS:
Identify and comment on the writer's purpose and point of view, and the overall effect of the text on the reader.

- The purpose of the opening sentence is to create interest and draw the reader into the rest of the article.
- It is effective because it:
  - takes the reader straight to the scene 'we are in' by using the first person;
  - creates an intriguing image through the metaphor of the taxi being 'a bouncy castle on wheels', making the reader want to know more;
  - uses interesting words such as 'a battered old silver Merc taxi';
  - adopts a humorous approach to the subject rather than simply describing where he is.

(1 mark for purpose, 2 for effectiveness, such as the suggestions given here – total 3)

---

9 Add the following subheadings to the passage and give each a number 1–5 to show the correct order.

QUESTION FOCUS:
Identify and comment on structure, organisation of texts including grammatical features.

A	From clothing to ceramics	2
B	A night with the camels	3
C	A feast of fish	5
D	Rough ride to Paradise	1
E	Madness in Marrakech	4

(1 mark for each two correct answers – total 2)

---

10 In paragraph 5, beginning 'Fez was a half-day on the train' (line 43), what different impressions does the writer create of the city of Fez? Complete the following table by adding one more metaphor from paragraph 5 and explain how the choice of language in each phrase creates a picture of the medina.

QUESTION FOCUS:
Explain and comment on the writer's use of language and literary features.

Quotation/metaphor	The image that this metaphor creates for the reader
'kaleidoscopic maze'	brings out the variety of colours and shapes all crammed together so you can't tell where one stops and another begins
'swaddled by about one million narrow, winding, hilly lanes	suggests that the lanes are wrapped round the mosques like strips of cloth or binding tape
'storm of attention'	sums up the all enveloping noise and commotion of the shouting boys clamouring for attention, a bit like a thunderstorm

(1 mark for each of the first two explanations, 1 mark for giving the third metaphor, 1 for explaining the image it creates – total 3)

> **I I** Focusing only on the last section of the passage from line 75 onwards, beginning 'Another half-day in a first-class compartment', comment on how the writer conveys his thoughts and experiences to the reader.

In this last section of the article the writer creates a vivid impression of his experiences through his use of language and the images he creates. The following are some examples of the ways in which he engages the reader's attention. The writer:

- adopts a humorous tone by making comments such as: 'listening to the camels regurgitating what sounded like entire fields of shrubs';
- uses the simile 'Morocco in all its madness hits you like a lorry' – to emphasise the impact of the scene he is describing; a lorry is rather large and not something you could miss easily;
- humorously addresses the reader directly – 'in case you want to look like a human doodle'. Henna patterns have very complicated lines, which could look like doodles to those who don't know about them; the idea of humans being doodles is funny, as is the word 'doodle' itself;
- makes interesting comparisons – 'Essaouira has wood workshops the way some houses have mice' – where there is one mouse there will soon be many more; the comparison here with wood workshops is funny because it suggests they too breed rapidly;
- wittily uses personification to describe the carpentry – 'any self respecting tree would have been happy to have been turned into them' – which is continued in the idea that the trees would be happy to be sacrificed, chopped down and turned into a piece of elaborate Moroccan furniture;
- draws the article to a close by humorously describing how the argan seeds are collected – 'Not the sort of thing you put on the side of the bottle' – which sums up what the reader may be thinking. It is a funny comment to use at the end of the article but it helps the writer avoid the problem of a 'gushing' conclusion.

(I mark for giving a correct example, I for the comment or explanation (based on the type given above – to a total of 5)

Questions 12–14 are about *The Pocket Guide* **(pages 78–80**

12 How does the writer use punctuation to clarify meaning? Complete the following table.

QUESTION FOCUS: Identify and comment on the writer's purpose and point of view and the overall effect of the text on the reader

Punctuation feature	Example	How it helps the reader
dash	– a real delight for your taste buds. *line 27*	The dash allows the writer to informally add extra information to interest and speak to the reader directly.
inverted commas	'light snack' *line 47*	The inverted commas are used by the writer to suggest to the reader that although it may be called a light snack, it is in fact the opposite.
brackets	(meat, chicken, or fish stew with vegetables) *line 53*	The brackets are used by the writer to give the reader additional information.

(3 marks)

13 Are the following statements from the guide fact or opinion? Complete the following table.

QUESTION FOCUS: Deduce, infer, or interpret information, ideas or events.

Statement	Fact or opinion
A 'a country that is a feast for all the senses'	Opinion
B 'This is the very best of Oriental cuisine'	Opinion
C 'The day is marked by five calls to prayer'	Fact
D 'The folk dances are magnificent'	Opinion

(1 mark only if all answers are correct – total 1)

14 The purpose of this guide is to give travellers to Morocco information and advice about the country. Explain how the writer demonstrates an awareness of the reader's needs?

You should comment on:
- the writer's use of language;
- the structure and organisation of the information;
- the ways in which it has been made accessible.

The writer's use of language
The writer:
- persuades the reader through the use of vivid adjectives in the first paragraph – 'wonderful', 'spectacular' and 'most beautiful', creating a positive image of the country;
- creates an enticing mood of ancient mystery through the words 'century-old', 'eternal';
- uses the second person 'you' to speak to the reader directly in the second section;
- introduces Moroccan vocabulary to give a flavour of the local language, such as 'shebbakia', 'bismillah' and 'muezzin'.

The structure and organisation of the information
- The guide begins with a persuasive description of the country to entice the reader.
- The topics are chosen to reflect areas that will interest the reader because they may be different to their own country.
- There is a logical development from the country itself to the food (always a main concern) which leads to cultural areas of interest such as the way of life, which is related to religion and folklore.
- Short paragraphs are used on each topic so the reader can gain a flavour of what they need to know and then move on to the next topic.

The ways it has been made accessible
- Headings in a bold contrasting colour help the reader to see the topics covered quickly and easily.
- Narrow columns break down the content so it looks short and easy to read.
- Pictures provide interest and colour; they also illustrate the points made.
- Subheadings in the second section help the reader to find particular references to special foods easily.
- Bullet points in the third section make the list easy to read, like a checklist. They are also different to the rest of the text.

(1 mark for each point and comment, at least two from each section – total 5)

Writing Paper Answers and Guidance

Even your English teachers will agree that assessing writing isn't easy. There is more to good writing than telling a good story; similarly, writing that is error free may be dull in terms of content. Therefore, when assessing writing, a balance needs to be made between skill and content. The guidelines below will help you to understand how well you have done, as well as pinpointing weaknesses to help you improve.

After you have assessed your work, look back at those revision sessions in the 'Focus on Writing' section on pages 22-47 which are likely to help you improve your writing next time.

In the Writing Paper, the examiners will look at different aspects of your work, which are slightly different for the two sections (see the assessment charts below). The marks you gain for each assessment focus are added together to give an overall score out of 30 for the longer writing task and 20 for the shorter writing task.

How to assess your response to the longer writing task

For each assessment focus A – C, (see charts below) match your achievement against one of the statements; the one you think gives the 'best fit'. Put the mark you have scored in the final column. Add these marks together and you will have a score for this task as a whole.

The chart on page 103 can be used to give you an indication of your level. It is good idea to ask someone else for their opinion too.

Assessment Focus A: Sentence structure, punctuation and text organisation

How well do you use sentences and punctuation to interest and guide your reader? How well do you organise your writing so that it can be easily understood by the reader?	Mark awarded	Your mark
You write mostly simple sentences which are usually correctly punctuated using full stops and sometimes question marks and commas to show pauses. Sometimes conjunctions are used such as *and*, *but*, *so*. Sentence construction tends to be straightforward and repetitive – subject, verb, object.	0	
You write in sentences which may include using conjunctions such as *when*, *and*, *then*, *so* and subordinate clauses. You usually use commas to indicate phrases and full stops correctly. There is some variety in your sentence construction, such as beginning with an adverb: 'Suddenly he ran away'.	1–2	
You often use complex sentences in your writing, including, for example, connectives such as *because*, *if*, *when*, to make links between points. You also use modal (helper) verbs such as *could*, *might*, *should*. The word order of your sentences is varied, e.g. 'Sliding down the muddy bank…' Commas are usually used to separate clauses, and inverted commas for speech are mostly in place.	3–4	
Phrases and clauses are naturally used in your sentences to give readers more information. You vary your sentence length, such as by one word sentences, to create interest. A variety of punctuation marks, including all that is needed to write speech accurately, make your writing clear. You are beginning to use impersonal constructions such as 'It is often thought that …'	5–6	
Your sentences are naturally varied in length and construction, including phrases like 'After the trials of the day…' or questions to provoke thought. Deliberate effects are created by your accurate use of a variety of different types of punctuation, such as semi-colons to balance ideas. You can use personal and impersonal starting points.	7	
The varied length, range and focus of your sentences control the reader's pace and understanding. You create deliberate effects by using a variety of punctuation marks, e.g. dashes, brackets, pairs of commas, to suit an intended purpose such as emphasising a point. Your writing is controlled and interesting to read.	8	

Assessment Focus B: Structure and organisation

How well do you organise your writing? Do you sequence ideas and events logically? Are your paragraphs sensibly structured including openings, link sentences and endings?	Mark awarded	Your mark
Your writing has a straightforward structure where similar ideas are usually grouped together in paragraphs.	0	
You use paragraphs to group ideas together, to put events in order or to organise similar points. A topic sentence is often used to introduce the main idea or signal a change in topic.	1–2	
Your paragraphs help you to develop ideas. Following a topic sentence, relevant detail within the paragraph is given, leading to a summary or a link to the next paragraph.	3-4	
Your writing follows a clearly organised pattern that helps you to develop your ideas in a logical way and interest the reader. You develop paragraphs consistently, using topic sentences, followed by related detail and varied length.	5–6	
Your interesting introduction immediately gains the attention of the reader, maintained throughout your writing with its clear conclusion. The details within your paragraphs are well organised, often creating particular effects. You vary the length of your paragraphs to give your writing pace (speed it up or slow it down).	7	
Your paragraphs are deliberately controlled and structured in an appropriate way, to make the writing interesting and direct the reader's attention to particular points. You use a variety of strategies to connect your ideas logically, including referring to events that have happened or are still to come.	8	

Assessment Focus C: Composition and Effect

In this section you will need to decide whether you: just do this (lowest mark in the range); do it exactly; or do it well (highest mark in the range).

Far does your writing interest the reader? How well does it suit its intended purpose?	Mark awarded	Your mark
You show some understanding of the purpose and needs of the reader. You tell your story simply, with a few interesting details, but there is a lack of development in places. You use many pronouns (he/she/it/they/we) and ordinary verbs such as ran, eat, think, go, is, etc. Sometimes your style is too informal.	0	
Your writing shows an awareness of the reader through your chosen style. In places, you develop interesting ideas. You tend to use everyday words, but there are also glimpses of a more imaginative vocabulary. Your writing occasionally becomes too informal.	1–3	
At times your use of lively writing creates an interest for the reader. You use some unusual vocabulary, often choosing words to interest the reader, e.g. adjectives and adverbs to give finer detail. There is a definite imaginative storyline and your characters are beginning to be developed. Sometimes you over-use words such as 'and' or 'but', or clichés such as 'to be honest'; 'basically'; 'at this moment in time'.	4–6	
Your writing has a definite style and tone chosen to suit the subject and interest the reader, although it may not be continued throughout. You have organised your story with care, controlling events and developing characters to create an effect. You are aware that words need to be appropriate, and demonstrate a growing vocabulary, which together with features such as similes/metaphors, keep the reader interested.	7–9	
Your confident and well-crafted story is interesting to read. You use techniques such as starting at the end or in the middle of events, and select imaginative details for a purpose. Your words have been chosen deliberately to suit the purpose, create an effect and interest the reader. You use figurative language such as similes/metaphors/personification to contribute to the imaginative effect.	10–12	
Your writing imaginatively entertains the reader and you maintain an individual style right to the end. You use effective strategies, such as withholding information to create suspense or creating a twist in the tale. Your wide vocabulary is used to advantage ensuring that just the right effect is created. You use a full range of figurative language with ease.	13–14	

Give yourself a mark in each of these sections, then add up your marks to give you a total out of 30. This mark will be added together with your other marks from all the other papers. The total will then be translated into a level. Use the chart on page 103 to help you assess your level for the Writing Paper.

How to assess your response to the shorter writing task

The purpose of the shorter writing task is to show that you can write concisely in a particular form for a specific purpose and reader. You have less time to write than in the longer writing task, and therefore your writing therefore needs to be very focused and to the point. The way this task is marked gives extra credit for accurate spelling and the way you structure and use language in your writing to reflect the special requirements of the task.

It is assessed in a similar way to the longer task, except that there are fewer marks altogether and you will see that the focus of the sections is a little different. To do this, use charts D – F below. The principle of finding the 'best fit' description for your work in each section remains the same.

After you have assessed your work, look back at those revision sessions in the 'Focus on Writing' section on pages 48–61, which are likely to help you to improve your writing next time.

Assessment Focus D: Sentence structure, punctuation and text organisation

How well can you structure and organise your writing effectively in this short focused work?	Mark awarded	Your mark
You usually show where sentences begin and end using full stops and perhaps exclamation marks. Your sentences have a simple construction, 'I think fortune tellers are…', sometimes using simple connectives such as *and*, *but*, *so*.	0	
Your ideas are expressed in sentences that are sometimes varied in structure, using connectives such as *because*, *although*, *who* and *which*. You usually build paragraphs around topic sentences to help you to put your ideas in order. You often use capital letters, full stops and commas correctly.	1–2	
You vary the length of your sentences, including a range of connectives to help you to make your points clearly. Your paragraphs are correctly structured so you can easily move from one idea to another. Your punctuation within sentences, e.g. commas, is effective if limited in variety.	3–4	
You consciously use a variety of different types of sentence to create interest. This may include using words such as *would*, *could*, *might*, as well as changing the tense when it is appropriate. You are beginning to use a wider range of punctuation such as semi-colons, paired commas, question marks, correctly.	5	
You effectively select different types of sentence purposefully to create a deliberate effect, which includes changing the normal word order, as well as using short and long sentences effectively to create emphasis. You use the full range of punctuation accurately to make your points clear to the reader.	6	

Assessment Focus E: Composition and Effect

How far does your writing create an impact on the reader that suits the form and purpose of the task you were given?	Mark awarded	Your mark
You show that you are aware of the reader through the tone that you have used. Your writing may become too chatty or lacking in detail. There is not much content.	0	
You have generally written in a style that is appropriate for the purpose and the reader, but may sometimes be too informal. You are aware that you need to organise your ideas and support the points that you make with arguments. You have tried to persuade your reader to your point of view.	1–3	
You have written clearly in a style and tone that suits your reader and the purpose. You present your ideas in a consistent and persuasive way, making references to interesting points. In places you engage the reader through devices such as rhetorical questions and addressing him/her directly.	4–6	
Your style suits the task and engages the reader through your use of a range of persuasive devices. Your clear structure presents your interesting and sensible ideas, which are well supported by evidence. You use stylistic devices, such as contrast and good humour, to make your case persuasively, without lapsing into an inappropriate tone.	7–9	
You show a confident awareness of your reader through your style and tone, using language that will appeal, without being too informal. You have logically structured your points to persuade and provide information, using a full range of devices to create effects. Overall, there is a professional feel to the finished piece that inspires trust in the message you are giving.	10	

Assessment Focus F: Spelling

How accurate is your spelling?	Mark awarded	Your mark
You spell simple and common words correctly, but you sometimes: • confuse words that sound the same e.g. break/brake; weather/whether • leave out syllables in longer words e.g. rember for remember; • make mistakes when changing a word e.g. cryed/ cried; leafs/leaves	1	
You spell complex common and regular words correctly, but have problems when you: • add a suffix, e.g. respectible/respectable; beautyful/ beautiful • use hyphens incorrectly, e.g. class-room; guide-book; grand-daughter (which shouldn't have hyphens)	2	
You spell most complex and irregular words correctly; some errors you may make could include: • unstressed vowels e.g. independant/ independent; seperate/separate • doubling consonants e.g. neccessary/necessary; occassion/ocassion	3	
Your spelling is almost perfect apart from the odd slip up, which doesn't happen more than two or three times in your writing.	4	

When you have finished assessing your work, add up the marks you have given yourself to make a total out of 20. This mark will be added to those for your other papers to give a final total, which is then translated into a level.

Use the chart on page 103 to help you assess your level for the Writing Paper.

Reading and Writing:
How to Assess your Level

Use the chart below to help you assess your level.

Remember that this is only part of the whole picture that will lead to your final level. In particular, there is your response to the question on your Shakespeare play, which we have not covered here. If you wish to include this element in your assessment, you should consult the appropriate section in *Collins Test Practice KS3 English.*

The following chart is a rough guide to help you assess your level for the Reading and Writing Papers. The actual boundary marks between levels vary slightly from year to year, depending on the difficulty of the papers set.

Level	Reading Paper	Writing Paper Section A (Longer Task)	Writing Paper Section B (Shorter Task)	Total (excluding the Shakespeare Paper)
3	1–4	1–3	1	1–10
4	5–9	4–8	2–4	11–23
5	10–15	9–14	5–8	24–39
6	16–21	15–20	9–12	40–55
7	22–32	21–30	13–20	56–82

HOW WELL HAVE YOU DONE?

Reading skills answers and guidance

Use this section to check the answers you gave to the tasks and questions in the 'Focus on Reading' section on pages 2–21.

REVISION SESSION 1

(pages 2–3)

---

1 Create a 'Fact File' giving information about the Takla Makan Desert.

This is how your chart should look:

Fact File on the Takla Makan Desert	
Number of days taken crossing the desert:	26 days
Lowest night-time temperature:	35 degrees Fahr.
General sky conditions – night:	Clear, no clouds
General sky conditions – day:	Clear, no clouds
Wind strength:	0, no wind

(total 2 marks)

---

2 Describe Hedin's journey on May 7th in no more than 40 words.

Stage 1: These are the facts that you should have highlighted in the text on page 3.

- I now changed my course to due south-east.
- the moon was a silver crescent in that quarter of the sky, shedding a dim, pale blue illumination
- I plodded away at a steady pace in a straight line towards the south-east
- At intervals I was seized by a desire to sleep, and was obliged to stop and rest.
- My pulse was excessively weak
- I had to steel myself to prevent myself dropping off to sleep.
- I walked with my eyes riveted upon the moon.
- The whole of the east quarter was enshrouded in the cool night mist.

Stage 2: Your short list of the facts could look like this:

- walked steadily due south-east
- moon provided light
- rested but no sleep
- weak pulse
- cool mist

(15 words)

Stage 3: Your final answer can now be expanded slightly, using the third person:

> Hedin, walking steadily and straight, changed course to due south-east. A crescent moon provided light as he walked. He stopped to rest, because his pulse was weak, but he did not sleep. From the east came a cool night mist.

(40 words exactly – total 5 marks)

REVISION SESSION 2

(pages 4–7)

I From the extract what do you learn about the conditions and setting in which the boy was making his journey? Give two examples from the text and explain what each tells us.

Example: 'a huge stone precipice rose up ahead of him'
Explanation: As he went on he was faced by a large cliff of rock, which he knew he wouldn't be able to climb.

Example: 'It seemed to grow bigger with each step he took.'
Explanation: This tells us that as he walks towards the rock he realises that it is much larger than he thought it was when he was further from it.

(1 mark for each example, 1 for the explanation – total 4 marks)

2 Look at the section 'And he knew he'd never be able to climb it...' to '...he didn't know if he'd even try'. What do we learn about the boy's physical and emotional condition?

Physical condition: In this section we learn that the boy's climb makes him thirsty, he starts thinking about water, but when it says, 'he knew he wouldn't find water', we know he thought he wouldn't find water at the top of the huge rock.

Emotional condition: We can tell that the boy begins to lose hope when it says, 'It was the bitter smell of despair.' This seems to be an echo of his own feelings, he is desperate to find water, but doesn't think he will.

Or: We can tell that in spite of all his problems, the boy is also very determined, which is shown when it says, 'If nothing else, he wanted to at least reach the Thumb.'

(1 mark for each correct example and comment – total 4 marks)

3 **Explain why, when Zero asks what he is being given to eat at the end of the extract, Stanley replies, 'A hot fudge sundae.'**

Sample answer

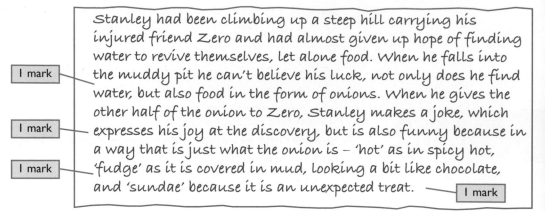

Stanley had been climbing up a steep hill carrying his injured friend Zero and had almost given up hope of finding water to revive themselves, let alone food. When he falls into the muddy pit he can't believe his luck, not only does he find water, but also food in the form of onions. When he gives the other half of the onion to Zero, Stanley makes a joke, which expresses his joy at the discovery, but is also funny because in a way that is just what the onion is – 'hot' as in spicy hot, 'fudge' as it is covered in mud, looking a bit like chocolate, and 'sundae' because it is an unexpected treat.

1 mark

1 mark

1 mark

1 mark

(total 4 marks)

REVISION
SESSION **3**

(pages 8–11)

2 Explain the purpose and effect of the following punctuation marks used by the writer:

(a) The dash in line 4 'and damage crops – an extraordinary episode'.

The dash is used in this sentence to add a comment about the main point rather like an afterthought. The effect of the dash is to link in this comment in a casual way but giving greater status than it would have if brackets were used.

(b) The inverted commas around the word 'harmless' in the last line of the third paragraph.

The inverted commas here indicate that the chemicals may be labelled as harmless, but in fact they obviously are not. Inverted commas show the author's doubt and distrust of the word.

(1 mark for each correct answer – total 2 marks)

3 Comment on the effect and purpose of the questions used in the extract below:

What other parallels may there be, not only in Colorado but wherever chemical pollution finds its way into public waters? In lakes and streams everywhere, in the presence of catalysing air and sunlight, what dangerous substances may be born of parent chemicals labelled 'harmless'?

> The writer uses rhetorical questions, not expecting any answers, but to make the reader think about the issues raised. They help to create a feeling of doubt in the reader's mind about the safety of the chemicals.

(1 mark for 'rhetorical', 1 for commenting on their effect – total 2 marks)

4 Explain how the writer uses the opening sentence of each paragraph as signals to the reader.

Paragraph 1: 'It must have been by such a dark, underground sea that poisonous chemicals travelled from a manufacturing plant in Colorado…'

> The words 'It must have been by such a dark, underground sea' create a powerful image of malevolence that draws the reader into the paragraph's topic of how poisonous chemicals can travel underground.

Paragraph 2: 'The irrigation waters on these farms were derived from shallow wells.'

> The writer quickly establishes the topic of the paragraph through the opening words of the first sentence, 'The irrigation waters'.

Paragraph 3: 'And so the story of the Colorado farms and their damaged crops…'

> The words 'And so the story' at the beginning of the paragraph signals that the 'story' that she has been telling about water pollution is coming to an end. This sentence links the new paragraph with previous ones and begins to make summary points.

Paragraph 4: 'Indeed, one of the most alarming aspects of the chemical pollution…'

> The writer's use of the word 'indeed' here acts as a signal to show that she is introducing a final comment drawn from the points made in previous paragraphs.

(1 mark for a correct comment on each of the four paragraphs – total 4 marks)

1 (a) Which of the following do you think best sums up what the writer is saying? (underline your choice)
(b) Find another quotation that makes a negative comment about Scotland's weather in a similar tone.

(a) You should have underlined:

Cycling in Scotland is only for those who are devoted to the sport.

(1 mark)

(b) Another quotation that makes a negative comment about Scotland's weather in a similar tone: 'the worst rain, snow and sleet that Scotland can throw at you.'

(1 mark)

2 'they snake beneath thick forest canopies' *(paragraph 2)*
Comment on the imagery the author has chosen to use here.

The word 'snake', used here to describe the bicycle tracks, is an appropriate image because they are in a forest and snakes can be found in forests. It also suggests that the tracks wind and slither through the trees. 'Forest canopies' suggests that the high tree tops act like an awning to shelter the riders.

(1 mark for commenting on each of the two images – total 2 marks)

3 'Red Bull has recently completed a new downhill course for mountain bikers who require such things as 14ft drop-offs to have a good day in the country.' *(end of the third paragraph)*
(a) Explain the writer's sense of humour in this sentence.

1 mark

The writer has already suggested that bikers have rather strange ways to enjoy themselves by going out in the cold and rain. The comment 'mountain bikers who require 14ft drop-offs to have a good day in the country' continues the idea, this time suggesting that they are also quite keen on taking great risks with their lives. His flippant comments suggest there is something brave but very odd about this form of entertainment. The contrast creates the humour.

1 ma

(1 mark for each point made to explain the humour – total 2 marks)

(b) Find another example of the writer's humour.

- 'there's a reasonable amount of trees for a start'
- 'where there's a hose to clean your bike and maybe yourself'
- 'and the views aren't bad either'
- 'But how about a ski lift to the top?'

(any one of the above quotations will earn you 1 mark)

4 'intimidatingly steep descents' *(in the seventh paragraph)*

You should have underlined <u>threateningly</u> (intimidate means to threaten someone).

(1 mark)

5 Examine the paragraph that begins 'So what are the new trails like?' How does the author persuade the reader that these trails would be worth visiting?

1 mark

1 mark

The writer begins by asking a question to draw the reader in, and he then proceeds to give them an answer. He uses a chatty, informal tone, for example 'Well' and 'for a start', to sound as if he is a friend talking to us personally. Later he describes the trails using words and phrases such as 'superb', 'easily forgotten' and 'sweeping views across the wild, open moorland', which persuade us that they are worth the visit, because he makes them sound wonderful.

1 mark

1 mark

(1 mark for each point, plus 1 for addressing the overall question at the end – up to 4 marks. Note the way in which each point is supported by evidence, a quotation and a comment)

6 Explain why you think 'Break for the Borders' is a suitable and effective title for this article.

In your answer you would need to make any two points from the following list:

- The alliteration of the letter 'b' will attract the reader (it is also the same letter that 'bicycle' begins with).
- There is a play on the word 'break', meaning take a break – a holiday – and the idea of a bicycle 'brake', needed when going down the Scottish hills.

(continued)

- The writer later talks about 'wide-open fire roads' or 'breaks' in the trees down which you can cycle freely.
- The 'borders' in the title refers to the area of Scotland near to the border with England. There is another play on the word here too because the cycle routes are down the borders between the trees in the forest – he mentions, for example, 'ruler-edge boundaries'.
- The tone of the title is catchy and informal, which is reflected in the style of the article itself.

(1 mark for each point – total 2 marks)

REVISION SESSION 5

(pages 18–21)

> **1 Discuss the effect created by the poet's image of the trees in the first stanza, including her use of figurative language.**

In this stanza the poet has used personification to strengthen the empathy that the reader feels for the tree. She begins 'The sore trees', which suggests that they are in pain, causing them to cast off the burden of their leaves before their time.

She uses a simile to describe the twigs 'pinching shut like a clam' to emphasise the sudden, tight closing down of the twigs as if they have been 'jabbed', struck again in pain.

Finally there is an unusual contrast in the image 'a hot gauze of snow searing the roots.' Nature has been turned upside down, so that normally cold snow has become hot, 'searing' instead of freezing the roots. This creates a frightening image of a natural world we don't understand.

(1 mark for explaining the effect of each image – total 3 marks)

> **2 (a) What effect does the verb 'wrecked' in the last line of the second stanza create?**

Either: The word 'wrecked' reminds us of shipwrecks and suggests that the tadpoles have been left stranded on the shore or the rocks and left to die.
Or: 'Wrecked' suggests that the tadpoles' lives have been destroyed, they lie wasted and dead, perhaps deformed by the pollution.
Or: 'Wrecked' is a slang term for drunk which picks up the other images of drunkenness – 'frogless' (legless), 'booze', 'pure antifreeze', 'drunk'. It suggests that the tadpoles are helplessly drunk, but the twist is that their intoxication is real and deadly.

(1 mark for any of these answers)

(b) *'You would if.'* **What is the purpose of this last line of the third stanza?**

The poet leaves us with an unfinished thought in this line, because what she would say, if she was to finish it, is almost too terrible to think about. She is suggesting that we would cook and eat the eel with an eye coming from its cheek, if there was nothing else to eat, and without it we would starve.

(1 mark for each point – total 2 marks)

3 Explain how the last stanza helps you to understand why the poet has written this poem.

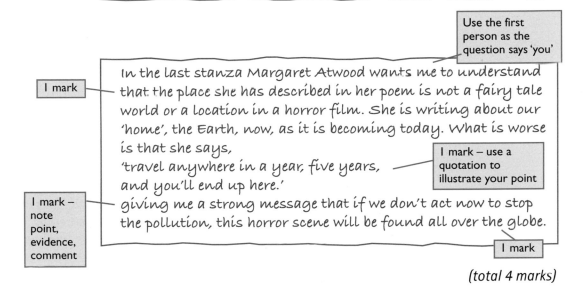

Use the first person as the question says 'you'

I mark

In the last stanza Margaret Atwood wants me to understand that the place she has described in her poem is not a fairy tale world or a location in a horror film. She is writing about our 'home', the Earth, now, as it is becoming today. What is worse is that she says,
'travel anywhere in a year, five years, and you'll end up here.'
giving me a strong message that if we don't act now to stop the pollution, this horror scene will be found all over the globe.

I mark – use a quotation to illustrate your point

I mark – note point, evidence, comment

I mark

(total 4 marks)

Writing skills answers and guidance

Use this section to check the answers you gave to the tasks and questions in the 'Focus on Writing' section on pages 22–61.

REVISION SESSION 1

(pages 22–25)

1 START YOUR SENTENCES IN AN INTERESTING WAY (page 22)

(a) The librarian put the books back on the shelf fussily.

New versions you may have written:
• *Fussily the librarian put the books back on the shelf.*
• *Putting the books back on the shelf, the librarian fussed.*
• *Back onto the shelf went the books as the librarian fussed.*

(b) The bird flew high into the sky and sang a song of joy.

New versions:
• *Flying high into the sky, the bird sang a song of joy.*
• *Singing a song of joy, the bird flew high into the sky.*
• *High into the air flew the bird, singing a song of joy.*

2 USE A MIXTURE OF SIMPLE, COMPLEX AND COMPOUND SENTENCES (page 23)

Here are some examples of how to make the sentences complex or compound:

(a) The bus was very late.
Complex sentence: The bus, *caught in a traffic jam*, was very late.
(a subordinate clause has been added, no active verb here)
Compound sentence: The bus was very late, *because there was a traffic jam*.
(a second main clause has been added, containing an active verb – *was*)

(b) Granny glared irritably at the shop assistant.
Complex sentence: Granny, *deeply upset by the remark*, glared irritably at the shop assistant. (a subordinate phrase has been added, no active verb)
Compound sentence: Granny glared irritably at the shop assistant, *who had made a remark that upset her*. (a second main clause containing an active verb – *made*)

4 UNDERSTAND HOW AND WHEN TO USE QUESTIONS AND EXCLAMATIONS (page 24)

Here are some examples – make sure you have added a question mark:
1 Do you know how many fleas *there are on my cat?*
2 Have you ever thought about *how birds can fly?*
3 What sort of person would *kick an animal?*

5 LEARN HOW TO WRITE SPEECH CORRECTLY (page 25)

Check that in your conversation you have:
• started a new line with each new speaker;
• used inverted commas around the words that are spoken;
• punctuated the sentences according to the normal guidelines;
• made it clear who is speaking.

Bonus points if you have:
- varied the words used to introduce the speaker, such as 'responded', 'enquired', 'muttered';
- interspersed speaking with description or action of the characters;
- used adverbs such as 'quietly', 'hurriedly', 'crisply' to describe how the words are spoken.

(pages 26–29)

Further annotations about paragraphs and organisation of the extract on page 27:

Paragraph 2 – opening is a topic sentence as the rest of the paragraph is about saying goodbye to people who had looked after Mandela in prison.

Paragraph 3 – 'By 3.30' signals a change in events. It also increases pace as a reminder of time passing. Final sentence links the new topic to the next paragraph.

Paragraph 5 – First sentence picks up the link introduced in the previous paragraph. The final sentence concludes the description contained in the paragraph as a whole.

Paragraph 6 – Topic change to focus on feelings as the writing is brought to a conclusion, which is enhanced by a strong final sentence summarising the whole extract.

(pages 30–33)

TASK I (page 31)
The words underlined would be the best replacement for those in the paragraph. (Note: where more than one word is suitable, the other choices are in brackets):

    small: tiny diminutive unimportant <u>little</u> miniature
    land: (<u>ground</u>) territory place (<u>soil</u>) <u>earth</u>
    fields: <u>countryside</u> territory (<u>grassland</u>) area (<u>meadows</u>)
    brown: chocolate russet brunette (<u>bronzed</u>) <u>tanned</u>
    painful: throbbing (<u>anguished</u>) excruciating (<u>burning</u>) <u>agonizing</u>

TASK 2 (page 31)
The paragraph could be improved by replacing these five words:

	Word from the extract:		Replacement:
I	farming		agriculture
2	people		citizens
3	good		beneficial
4	country's		nation's
5	bad		adverse

TASK A (page 32)
The language of the extract is far too wordy and difficult for young people. You would definitely need to:
- change words such as: flora; fauna; jeopardy; criteria; fragmented population; liable; susceptible; vulnerable; organisms; enduring
- make the tone far more user-friendly in order to attract younger readers

Here is an example of what it could be like:

> Some plants and animals are dying out. They may be called 'endangered' if it looks as if they could become extinct and disappear altogether. If this is happening to them they could fit into one or more of the following groups...

TASK B (page 33)

The language here is far too informal and 'chatty' in tone. It sounds more like a persuasive advertisement than an information text. You should have:

- turned the question at the beginning into a statement;
- changed informal words such as crystal-clear, roundabout, jaunt, chomped;
- written although, not tho';
- replaced clichés such as rumour has it; mega expensive; word is that; greedy glutton

Here is an example of what it could be like:

In England growing melons is a relatively new venture, but they have been grown in France for centuries. It is not clear when exactly they were first cultivated. 1495 is the first recorded date...

REVISION SESSION 4

(pages 34–37)

There were many tasks and explorations linked with spelling strategies in this section – but you know that the best place to find the answers is in your dictionary! The answers will all be in there and you are more likely to remember how to spell words if you have to do a bit of hard work first!

REVISION SESSION 5

(pages 38–39)

The corrections that you should have made to the extract are as follows:

Better without the 'and'

...Suddenly Chris didn't know where ~~were~~ to turn. The streets all looked the same, ~~and~~ the buildings ~~towared~~ towered above him. He ~~tries~~ tried to look at his map, but the writing was too small and in any case the words seemed so strange he couldn't hold them in his head. The noise around him was increasing. People were calling out prices; ~~gossipping~~ gossiping in corners; ~~and their was~~ a busker was hammering out a tune somewhere in the distance.

Semi-colons used as in this list make the description sharper

Note the effect of emphasis created by putting these questions in a separate paragraph

NP What should he do? Where should he go~~,~~?

NP He ~~I~~ decided to try again and see if ~~someone spoke any~~ anyone could speak English. He went to a flower stand a little apart from the others, on the edge, by the water.

In spite of all the confusion he felt within himself, Chris

couldn't help noticing the ~~chearful~~ *cheerful* colours of the flowers –

crimson and indigo   *gold*   *sunlight*
~~reds and blues~~, ~~whites and yellows~~ – dancing in the ~~sun light~~.

For a moment he stood looking at them, forgetting his troubles.

<u>NP</u> Suddenly there was a shout from the woman next to him.

She started shouting something in French. ~~and~~ *He* ~~he~~ didn't

understand what she was saying, but it didn't sound very

She   *pointing*
pleasant. ~~and she~~ kept ~~point~~ at him, ~~and~~ shaking her finger...

REVISION SESSION 6

(pages 40–41)

HOW DO WRITERS CREATE CHARACTERS?
(page 40)

Writers create characters by:
- the things they say to others
- their thoughts
- their actions
- what other people say about them

DESCRIBING A CHARACTER (page 41)

Look at the difference you can create with just two sentences describing your character. Approaches like these don't take long but will help to bring the person alive for the reader:

> Although tall, Chris looked young for his age. His fair hair stuck out at different angles from his head, giving him the unkempt look of a boy who would be happier in the fields than on the streets of a foreign city.

Or perhaps:

> In his smart clothes, looking every bit the city 'slicker', Chris had an air of confidence, older than his years. His bright eyes matched his relaxed smile and it was easy to see why he was popular at school.

CREATING A PERSON THROUGH THEIR THOUGHTS AND ACTIONS (page 41)

You can create tension and interest through the thoughts and actions of your character, as the examples below demonstrate:

Chris scanned the square, and seeing no one he recognised, realised that he had been left behind...

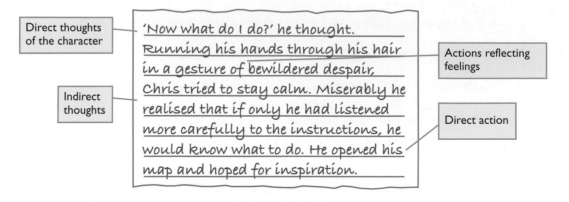

Direct thoughts of the character

Indirect thoughts

'Now what do I do?' he thought. Running his hands through his hair in a gesture of bewildered despair, Chris tried to stay calm. Miserably he realised that if only he had listened more carefully to the instructions, he would know what to do. He opened his map and hoped for inspiration.

Actions reflecting feelings

Direct action

REVISION SESSION 7

(pages 42–43)

MAKING AN IMPRESSIVE START (page 42)

Order of merit for the extracts (1 being the best) is as follows:

1 **extract 4** – imaginative approach, varied sentence length, interesting vocabulary such as 'sucked into their midst'
2 **extract 3** – begins at a definite, exciting point, sentence structure used well
3 **extract 1** – draws reader in through question, good vocabulary, e.g. 'lured'
4 **extract 2** – dull, starts too far back, nothing of interest here, not even vocabulary

If the writing in these opening paragraphs is sustained throughout the story, they would roughly achieve the following levels:

* Extract 4 has the potential to be a top level 7, but needs to maintain style.
* Extract 3 could achieve level 6, but needs a greater range of vocabulary to prevent it from becoming a level 5.
* Extract 1 could achieve a top level 6 (better than extract 3) because, although the opening is not as strong, a greater control of sentence structure and vocabulary is used to create effects.
* Extract 2 looks as if it will remain a level 4 unless something drastic happens to improve the content, structure and vocabulary.

TASK A (page 42)
Beginning your story – how well did you do?
Look at the beginning of your story and check that it:
* begins at a significant point;
* draws your reader into the story;
* introduces the context and character(s);
* is written in a style that is continued in the rest of the story.

A really good beginning will:
- create an impact on the reader;
- use varied sentence construction;
- have an interesting vocabulary.

A weak beginning will:
- take a long time to get to the point;
- be vague, confusing or too detailed;
- fail to fit in with the story that follows.

Capture the interest of the reader by:	
Starting at a significant point that creates an immediate impact	3
Creating a sense of mystery that makes the reader want to read on	1, 4
Using an interesting variety of words that sound appealing	4, 2
Making the subject of your writing clear in the first few sentences	3, 1, 4
Varying the length of your sentences to create an effect	4, 1, 3
Beginning with a conversation that generates interest in a situation	none
Having an unusual approach that will intrigue the reader	4, 3
Acknowledging the reader in some way, such as asking a question	1

CREATING A SUCCESSFUL ENDING (page 43)

Questions you could have asked:
- Does he find himself in a dangerous situation?
- Does he learn something from his experience?
- Does he get into trouble for getting himself lost?
- Does something good come from his adventure?
- Does he feel foolish because other people have taken advantage of him?
- Does he regret what happened to him?

Type		Extract
4 sad	Although he was glad to be back with his friends, Chris was sorry…	2
3 mystery	The image of the old woman haunted Chris as he closed his eyes…	4
2 narrator	Despite all that had happened, Chris was glad he had been lost…	1
1 twist	Aching limbs. Empty, growling stomach. Chris stared vacantly…	3

TASK B (page 43)
Ending your story – how well did you do?

Look at the ending that you have written and check that it:
- draws together points you made earlier in the story;
- is in keeping with the characters and events in your story;
- satisfies your reader – answers questions they may have had;
- comes to a definite conclusion.

A really good ending will:
- give your reader something to think about;
- make a judgement or tell a moral to the tale;
- leave the reader wishing the story hadn't come to an end.

A weak ending will:
- just end the story in a dull, predictable way;
- be unrealistic, not fitting the story properly;
- sound as if you couldn't think of anything else to say;
- be sudden, as if you have run out of room.

(pages 44–45)

Narrative voice	Narrative perspective	Advantages	Disadvantages
First person (I)	told by yourself as yourself	You: • know what really happened • can give personal insights and reflections on events • can help your reader to see things through your eyes	You: • don't really know what other people felt • may be too personally involved to give an unbiased picture • may be too emotional
First person (I)	told by a character you have created	The character: • can speak to the reader directly • gives his/her first thoughts and feelings • can comment on what has happened from a personal perspective	The character: • doesn't know what else is happening or how people feel unless there are conversations/letters etc. • is at the centre of everything
Third person (he or she)	narrator who makes comments and addresses the reader directly	The narrator: • can speak directly to the reader • can show what is happening to several characters • can make links between events and people • can comment on whether something is right or wrong	The narrator: • interferes with the reader's knowledge of the characters • might tell us things we don't want to know about what is going to happen • can sound patronising • takes away the fantasy that the reader 'is there' too
Third person (he or she)	simply telling the story in the past tense	The reader: • is being told an anonymous story • can see what is happening to several characters • forms her/his own opinion of events and characters	The reader: • is more detached from characters in terms of understanding them fully through their thoughts • is less personally involved

EXPERIENCES AND FEELINGS (page 45)

Feelings that Chris might have experienced when he discovered he was on his own:

afraid	panic	excited	helpless	anxious
alarmed	flustered	agitated	frenzied	elated
apprehensive	concerned	loneliness		

Here is an example of how you could write about the feelings Chris has:

> Anxiously staring at the opened map, Chris felt an overwhelming sense of loneliness. Apprehension concerning the strangers around him made him feel helpless. With a creeping alarm, he realised there was no one he could turn to. He was on his own.

Adverbs to describe feelings

half-heartedly	uncertainly
cheerfully	thankfully
uneasily	joyfully
gratefully	seriously
miserably	dejectedly

REVISION SESSION 9

FOLLOWING THE 'GOLDEN RULES' FOR SPEECH (page 46)

(pages 46–47)

Rule	Finally Chris found someone who could speak good English, a student who said she was studying English at University.
5, 4, 2, 1	'One minute I was exploring the market, with my mates,' he explained calmly, 'and the next I was on my own.'
3, 2	The student looked concerned. 'Where was your group going to next?' she asked.
5, 4, 3, 2	Feeling a little foolish, Chris replied, 'It sounds daft, but I don't know. I was having a quiet kip when we were given the itinerary this morning on the coach.'
1, 2, 3	'What is a kip?' she enquired. 'That's a new word for me.'
2, 3, 4	'A kip is a snooze, a catnap, a doze, you know – forty winks and all that,' he teased. 'Only I wish I hadn't been having one this morning, or I wouldn't be in this mess now.'
5, 3, 2	The young woman looked desperately at her watch. 'I'm really sorry,' she gasped, 'but I've got to go now or I'll miss my driving lesson. Here's my mobile number, ring me if you don't have any luck finding your friends.'
	She handed Chris a scrap of paper and disappeared into the crowded street.

What your reader may have learnt about Chris from this dialogue:

1 He can be calm in a moment of crisis.
2 He feels foolish when admitting to his mistakes.
3 He has a sense of humour.
4 He likes teasing people.
5 He regrets his mistakes.

ASSESSING YOUR CONVERSATION (page 47)

Check that you have followed the 'golden rules' for writing dialogue on page 46.

• Give yourself a tick for every correct punctuation mark.
• Put a circle around places where you think you have made a mistake.
• Put a ? by any point where you are not sure what to do.

If you need further guidance, look at the way speech has been written in any novel or short story you can find.

Remember that to be good, conversation needs to serve a purpose in your writing. For example, it should:

• move the story on
• introduce other characters who create interest
• provide a contrast to descriptive passages
• tell your reader more about your characters from the words they use
• develop your characters from the way they interact with one another

In addition, speech is also a good way to introduce some humour into your story.

TASK (page 47)
Assessing your story

Once you have written the whole story, hopefully within the time allowance of 45 minutes, you need to think about how well you have done. Compare your own story about Chris with the one we have been developing in this section:

'Where is everyone?'
  Suddenly looking around the bright market place, Chris realised he was alone. His school friends had all disappeared. He looked about in panic and could only hear strange foreign-sounding words he could not understand. ~~What should he do now?~~
  'Now what do I do?' he thought. Running his hands through his hair in a gesture of bewildered despair, Chris tried to stay calm. Miserably he realised that if only he had listened more carefully to the instructions, he would know what to do. He opened his map and hoped for inspiration.   it
  Anxiously staring at ~~the opened map~~, Chris felt an overwhelming sense of loneliness. Apprehension concerning the strangers around him, made him feel helpless. With a creeping alarm he realised there was no one he could turn to. He was on his own.

Although tall, Chris looked young for his age. His fair hair struck out at different angles from his head, giving him the unkempt look of a boy who would be happier in the fields than on the streets of a foreign city.

~~Suddenly~~ Chris didn't know where to turn. The streets all looked the same and the buildings ~~towared~~ above him. He ~~tries~~ to look at his map, but the writing was too small and in any case the words seemed so strange he couldn't hold them in his head. The noise around him was increasing. People were calling out prices gossipping in corners and their was a busker hammering out a tune somewhere in the distance. What should he do? Where should he go? ~~I~~ decided to try again and see if anyone could speak English. Reluctantly, using his very basic French, Chris decided to ask someone if they had seen a group of English students. He nervously approached the busker on the edge of the square, but the man looked uneasy and moved away. He went to a flower stand a little apart from the others on the edge by the water.

In spite of all the confusion he felt within himself, Chris couldn't help noticing the cheerful colours of the flowers – ~~reds~~ and ~~blues~~, white and gold – dancing in the sun light. For a moment he stood looking at them, forgetting his troubles.

Suddenly there was a shout from the woman next to him. She started shouting something in French and he didn't understand what she was saying, but it didn't sound very pleasant and she kept point at him and shaking her finger.

Finally Chris found someone who could speak good English, a student who said she was studying English at University.

'One minute I was exploring the market, with my mates,' he explained calmly, 'and the next I was on my own.'

The student looked concerned. 'Where was your group going to next?' she asked.

Feeling a little foolish, Chris replied, 'It sounds daft, but I don't know. I was having a quiet kip when we were given the itinerary this morning on the coach.'

'What is a kip?' she enquired. 'That's a new word for me.'

'A kip is a snooze, a catnap, a doze, you know - forty winks and all that,' he teased. 'Only I wish I hadn't been having one this morning, or I wouldn't be in this mess now.'

The young woman looked desperately at her watch. 'I'm really sorry,' she gasped, 'but I've got to go now or I'll miss my driving lesson. Here's my mobile number, ring me if you don't have any luck finding your friends.'

She handed Chris a scrap of paper and disappeared into the crowded street.

Aching limbs. Empty, growling stomach. Chris stared vacantly. The sky, just dawning, lit the tops of towering buildings. How had he got here? Was his mind playing tricks on him? Was this real?

(margin annotations:) towered · tried · He · new paragraph · new paragraph · indigo · crimson

COMMENTS ON THE STORY

The mark scheme on pages 99–100 has been used to assess this piece of writing.

Section A: Sentence structure and punctuation

Sentences are varied and have, at times, been used to create deliberate effects, for example the use of short sentences to create pace and tension, compound sentences which give information. There is also evidence of a variety of sentence openers showing that the writer has thoughtful control over the writing, making the piece interesting to read. Speech has been punctuated accurately and a good range of punctuation marks have been used.

Mark: 6 out of 8

Section B: Structure and organisation

There is an interesting introduction which creates an impact. Paragraphs, which vary in length, have been used to structure the writing logically and give it pace. Changes suggested by later checking show the writer's awareness of how to create a better effect in the middle section. Although there is a clear conclusion, it seems a little rushed and out of place, which is a weakness.

Mark awarded: 6 out of 8

Composition and effect

A good beginning catches the attention of the reader, there is a feeling of urgency and panic, no time has been wasted in unnecessary details. The reader is also given a good idea of the character through brief description, as well as comments about his feelings. Further character development, through the conversation, also introduces some humour.

There is an attempt to create a setting through interesting description, using a fairly wide vocabulary. The vocabulary is quite wide ranging, using interesting words such as 'indigo' 'vacantly and 'bewildered' to describe scenes and develop the reader's awareness of the character.

Unfortunately the writer's conclusion, although thought-provoking, comes rather suddenly and seems disconnected with the rest of the story.

Mark awarded: 8 out of 14

Overall this writing would achieve a level 6.

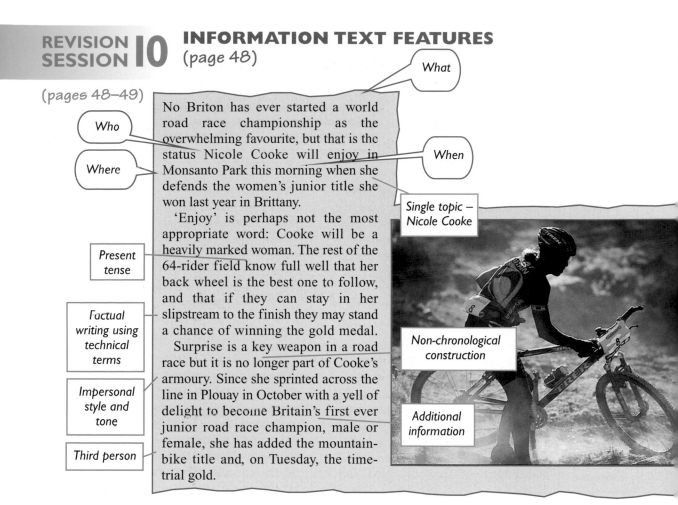

(pages 48–49)

What

Who

Where

When

No Briton has ever started a world road race championship as the overwhelming favourite, but that is the status Nicole Cooke will enjoy in Monsanto Park this morning when she defends the women's junior title she won last year in Brittany.

'Enjoy' is perhaps not the most appropriate word: Cooke will be a heavily marked woman. The rest of the 64-rider field know full well that her back wheel is the best one to follow, and that if they can stay in her slipstream to the finish they may stand a chance of winning the gold medal.

Surprise is a key weapon in a road race but it is no longer part of Cooke's armoury. Since she sprinted across the line in Plouay in October with a yell of delight to become Britain's first ever junior road race champion, male or female, she has added the mountain-bike title and, on Tuesday, the time-trial gold.

Single topic – Nicole Cooke

Present tense

Factual writing using technical terms

Impersonal style and tone

Third person

Non-chronological construction

Additional information

WRITING TASK: SPORTS FOR YEAR 9 STUDENTS (page 49)
How well have you done?

Use the charts on pages 101–102 to see how well you have done. In addition, consider the following points:

- Have you written in the third person?
- Have you used a formal, impersonal tone?
- Is your writing informative?

Remember, you are not selling anything and therefore your tone should not be persuasive.

Extract from a sample response:

> Sports for year 9 students at Westfield Community School are interesting and varied. The curriculum offers opportunities for those who enjoy both outdoor and indoor activities, team events and developing individual skills.
>
> There is a well-equipped gym, which is used for a variety of activities such as badminton, volleyball, and of course gymnastics. Students also enjoy the large indoor swimming pool all year round; boys and girls have lessons separately. However, outdoor sports, such as football in winter and cricket in summer, are played together.

General statement
to introduce topic

Logical, step by step
order, explaining process

Impersonal
voice

Present
tense

Title asking
a question to
be answered

Causal
connectives

Time
connective

Technical
terminology
explained

Complex
sentence

Gear Design

Some advantages of using gears to transmit forces, rather than other methods, include their small size and their ability to transmit large powers. On the other hand, gears are relatively expensive to make and require careful lubrication and protection from dirt.

How Do Gears Work?

One gear, called the driver, is meshed together with another, called the follower. When the driver is turned, the follower turns also. If the driver has 30 teeth, and the follower 60 teeth, then each time the driver turns twice the follower will turn only once. This means that the follower will turn at half the rate of the driver. The ratio between the speeds of the two wheels is called the velocity ratio. In this case the velocity ratio is 2. A velocity ratio greater than 1 means that a smaller effort at the input (the driver) can drive a larger load at the output (the follower), and the gears have a mechanical advantage.

When two gears are connected directly, the shafts rotate in opposite directions. A third wheel in the middle has no effect upon the overall velocity ratio, but causes the direction of rotation of the driven shaft to be reversed.

WRITING TASK: WHAT IS CONSERVATION?

(page 51)

How well have you done?

Use the charts on pages 101–102 to see how well you have done. In addition consider the following points:

- Does your leaflet explain the term 'conservation'?
- Have you set out your questions and answers clearly?
- Have you used the present tense?
- Have you written in an impersonal tone?

'Conservation' means protecting the earth's resources. It is important to everyone, because if these natural resources are not protected, someday they will run out.

How does conservation work?
If governments, and people all over the planet, take care with the natural resources that they use by reducing waste and re-using materials, then it will take longer for oil, coal and timber, to give a few examples, to run out. This will help to make the world a better place to live in...

How can individuals help?
People need to be aware that their individual actions have an effect on the environment as a whole. Every Coke can that is thrown away and not recycled means less aluminium for people in the future...

REVISION SESSION 12

(pages 52–53)

- Powerful nouns and verbs are underlined.
- Adjectives and adverbs are highlighted.
- Figurative language in italics has been annotated.

Metaphor to give the impression of the size and organisation of the penguin community

Baby penguins seen as fashionable young women about to be launched into society

This metaphor continues the image of the penguins looking like waiters

Ahead of us the low, brown <u>scrub</u> <u>petered out</u>, and in its place was a great desert of sun-cracked sand. This was separated from the sea beyond by crescent-shaped white sand dunes, very steep and some two-hundred feet high. It was in this desert area <u>protected</u> from the sea that the penguins had <u>created</u> their *city*. … In among these <u>craters</u> <u>waddled</u> the biggest collection of penguins I had ever seen, *like a sea of pigmy headwaiters,* solemnly <u>shuffling</u> to and fro *as if suffering from fallen arches due to a lifetime of carrying overloaded trays*. Their numbers were so prodigious, <u>stretching</u> to the furthermost <u>horizon</u> where they <u>twinkled</u> black and white in the heat haze. …

The greater proportion of birds were, of course, adult; but each nesting <u>burrow</u> contained two youngsters, still wearing their baby coats of down, who <u>regarded</u> us with big, melting dark eyes, *looking like plump, shy debutantes clad in outsized silver-fox furs.* The adults, sleek and neat in their *black and white suits,* had red <u>wattles</u> round the base of their beaks, and bright, *predatory, street peddler eyes.*

Simile links with ocean, creating image of numbers and size of penguins

Simile comparing penguins to old waiters with tired feet

Metaphoric image of penguins' eyes always on the lookout for trouble

WRITING TASK: DESCRIBE A JOURNEY (page 53)
How well have you done?

Use the charts on pages 101–102 to see how well you have done. In addition, give yourself a tick in the margin to show where you have:

- written in the first person
- written in the past tense
- described the train or boat itself
- mentioned points of interest that you saw on the way
- written about your feelings

Extract from a sample response:

> The ferry loomed above me, making me feel small and insignificant, like a sparrow peering up at a mansion. Its smell of oil and metal enveloped me. Strangely, it wasn't unpleasant, but added to the sense of adventure and excitement that I had for the journey.
>
> Once on board there were all kinds of places to explore. The wooden decks were brilliant – out there I felt like a voyager from long ago, smelling the sea and feeling the ship roll from side to side. The bleak coastline soon disappeared in the mist and then all that there was to see were a few squawking seagulls and the occasional distant fishing boat.

WRITING TASK: DESCRIBE YOUR SCHOOL (page 53)
How well have you done?

Use the charts on pages 101–102 to see how well you have done. In addition, give yourself a tick in the margin to show where you have:

- written in the third person
- written in the present tense
- described where your school is in the town
- described buildings and facilities
- described what it is like being a student in the school

Extract from a sample response:

> <u>Westfield Community School</u>
>
> On the western outskirts of the town, the school is built amongst new housing developments, surrounded by wide green playing fields that are used for football in winter and cricket in summer. It consists of several modern buildings spread out in a geometric pattern, interlinked by covered passageways and concrete courtyards.
>
> On school days there is a buzz of activity as students go from one lesson to another in their blue and black uniforms – sweatshirts and trousers. You can tell from the languages you hear in the playground that the school community comes from all over the world; in fact, eighteen different languages are spoken here and students come from over thirty different countries. Yet everyone feels at home – it's just a school like any other.

WRITING TO PERSUADE TASK (page 54)

> **10-point checklist for persuasive writing:**
>
> 1 Begin with an attention-catching opening statement or question.
> 2 Use appealing and persuasive adjectives to create an effect.
> 3 Connect ideas in a logical way.
> 4 Appeal to individuals directly by using 'you'.
> 5 Sound as if you are speaking personally to people by using 'my', 'I', 'me'.
> 6 Use the present tense for an immediate impact.
> 7 Give evidence to justify points made.
> 8 Use devices such as repetition, alliteration or rhetorical questions to reinforce what you are saying.
> 9 A formal tone used at the right time will sound convincing.
> 10 Link your conclusion with what you said at the beginning.

WRITING TASK: SUPERMARKET HANDOUT (page 55)

How well have you done?

Use the checklist above and put a tick in the margin of your work where you have followed this advice.

Extract from a sample response:

> Are you tired of eating the same old thing day in, day out?
>
> If you are, then we would like to offer you a very special, simple solution – a selection of treats from our freezers will brighten your dullest day. Our tempting assortment, Chinese and Indian, French and Italian, is waiting just for you – ready-cooked and mouthwateringly excellent! Be amazed by its variety.

PRESENTING AN ARGUMENT TASK (page 56)

Checklist of techniques:

1 Clearly state your point of view.
2 Adopt a formal tone.
3 Be impersonal – don't accuse anyone of anything.
4 Use persuasion to win people over to your point of view.
5 Present the opposite argument so you can show its weaknesses.
6 Appeal to people as reasonable human beings.
7 Use rhetorical questions.
8 Demonstrate that your argument is honest.
9 Develop your arguments in a logical way.
10 Assume your point of view to be a fact.

WRITING TASK: BANNING BICYCLES AT SCHOOL (page 57)

How well have you done?

Use the checklist above and put a tick in the margin of your work where you have followed this advice.

Extract from a sample response:

Headteacher, members of the school council, fellow students, in presenting my argument against the proposal to ban bicycles from the school premises, I would like you to consider the following points.

Firstly, it has been said that cycling to school is dangerous, because the roads around the school are busy with parents dropping off their children outside the gates. If this is true, then won't banning bicycles make the situation worse? I would like to suggest an alternative strategy which would ban parents in cars from coming within half a mile of the school, unless they have an appointment with a teacher. This would ease congestion and make the roads safer for cyclists.

WRITING TO ADVISE TASK (page 58)

Checklist for giving advice:

1 Gain the attention of your reader by appealing to them directly using 'you'.
2 Deal with points in a logical or chronological order.
3 Balance your tone between formal or informal so you don't sound threatening.
4 Gently dismiss bad ideas and show why they aren't sensible.
5 Make it sound as if many of your ideas are actually theirs.
6 Sound upbeat and convincing.
7 Give reasons why the advice should be followed.
8 Introducing some humour helps to decrease any tension.
9 Sound as if overcoming problems isn't difficult.
10 End on a positive note.

WRITING TASK: INFORMAL LETTER TO YOUR COUSIN (pages 59 and 60)

How well have you done?

Use the checklist for giving advice at the bottom of page 128 and put a tick in the margin of your work where you have followed this advice.

Extract from a sample response:

> 4 Beech Close
> Crompton
> CR4 5FJ
>
> 4 August 2004
>
> Dear Sarita,

> You will find that school canteens aren't very different in England. They are just as smelly and noisy as they are in India, only the type of food they serve is different. Don't think you can avoid the issue by not eating lunch, it will only cut you off from your new friends. Better to be brave and face it. You will probably know that some English people aren't too keen on spices, making their food rather bland, so my advice is to bring a jar of your favourite pickle with you – it will make anything taste good, even soggy cabbage!

REVISION SESSION 16

(pages 60–61)

WRITING TASK: FORMAL LETTER TO THE COUNCIL (page 61)

How well have you done?

Use the letter skeleton on page 61 and put a tick next to where you have followed this layout.

Extract from a sample response:

> 17 Brook Road
> Totton
> TR8 9QR
>
> Highways Officer
> Highways Department
> Totton District Council
> Town Hall
> High Street
> Totton TR4 8JP
>
> 3 June 2004
>
> Dear Sir,
>
> On behalf of my grandfather I am writing to complain about the general state of the pavements in Totton High Street. Litter seems to accumulate week after week without ever being cleared and the dangerous broken paving slabs make walking hazardous.
>
> Totton High Street is an area my grandfather visits every day to do his shopping and he is very worried about tripping on the broken slabs. If he injured himself he would not be able to look after himself as he does now. Becoming a burden on the community is something he fears. Repairing the pavements would be a small cost compared with the cost of treating injuries caused by neglect.

> Yours faithfully,
> K. Green
> Katy Green

Use this section to check the answers you gave to the tasks and questions in the 'Focus on Shakespeare' section on pages 62–71.

REVISION SESSION ▌

(pages 62–65)

MACBETH (pages 63–65)

Comments you could have made about the highlighted words and phrases on the extract below.

Act 1, Scene 7, lines 45–59

MACBETH Prithee, peace:
I dare do all that may become a man;
Who dares do more is none.

LADY MACBETH What beast was't, then,
That made you break this enterprise to me?
When you durst do it, then you were a man;
And, to be more than what you were, you would
Be so much more the man. Nor time nor place
Did then adhere, and yet you would make both:
They have made themselves, and that their fitness now
Does unmake you. I have given suck, and know
How tender 'tis to love the babe that milks me:
I would, while it was smiling in my face,
Have pluck'd my nipple from his boneless gums,
And dash'd the brains out, had I so sworn as you
Have done to this.

Macbeth, tired of her criticisms, declares he is the bravest of men

Shows she is not without humanity and feelings

She provokes and taunts Macbeth again, challenging him

Terrible contrast to what she has just said – horrifying image

---

Your own annotations of the third extract could look like this:

Act 5, Scene 1, lines 22–37

Doctor You see, her eyes are open.

Gentlewoman Ay, but their sense is shut.

Doctor What is it she does now? Look, how she rubs her hands.

Gentlewoman It is an accustomed action with her, to seem thus washing her hands: I have known her continue in this a quarter of an hour.

LADY MACBETH Yet here's a spot.

Doctor Hark! she speaks: I will set down what comes from her, to satisfy my remembrance the more strongly.

LADY MACBETH Out, damned spot! out, I say! – One: two: why, then, 'tis time to do't. – Hell is murky! – Fie, my lord, fie! a soldier, and afeard? What need we fear who knows it, when none can call our power to account? – Yet who would have thought the old man to have had so much blood in him?

She is not aware of what is going on around her, but also she cannot face the truth of her guilt

She seems to do this often

Illustrates her real fear of God's punishment

Again a reminder of Duncan, but also a metaphor – her sin has come back to haunt her and she now feels guilt

She seems to be awake. This is dramatic irony – she can now see the evil she has done earlier and feels the guilt

Mimics the action of washing or cleaning

She has found a stain – a mark on her conscience

Something she wants to get rid of

Reminders of Duncan's murder

WRITING A RESPONSE TO TASK I (pages 63, 65)

> **TASK I   Macbeth**
>
> *Act 1, Scene 6, lines 10–30; Act 1, Scene 7, lines 45–73; Act 5, Scene 1, lines 22–37*
>
> **Compare and contrast the impression created by Lady Macbeth in these extracts, through her words and actions.**

The sample response on page 65 could have been completed using the points, evidence and comments added below:

Lady Macbeth is an interesting central character in 'Macbeth'. At the beginning of the play, the way she uses situations to her advantage and changes her character tells us she manipulates people, such as Duncan and Macbeth, who she sees as weaker than herself. She is also clever and cunning, planning a murder for her husband to perform. In contrast, by the end of the play, she is a very different character, troubled by guilt and haunted by the past.

> Note how a brief outline has been given of the points to be made later in the essay.

In the first extract Lady Macbeth is shown to be dishonest and insincere through her flattery of the King. For example when Duncan arrives at the castle she tricks him into believing she is his 'honoured hostess', willing to do everything in her power to make his stay pleasant, 'All our service', from 'Your servants ever', when in fact she is planning to kill him. To make him unaware of her evil plans, she flatters him:

'Against those honours deep and broad wherewith
Your majesty loads our house:'

which illustrates her insincerity and dishonesty. For the audience there is also a cunning dramatic irony here, since we know she really is grateful that he has played into their hands by coming to their castle to meet his death.

> Look at the way quotations – short and long – have been used to support the points being made. There is also an awareness of the audience's point of view.

From this we can see that other characters find her charming and courteous, the ideal wife supporting her husband in his new role as Thane of Cawdor. Duncan calls her 'Fair noble hostess' and ironically takes her hand as they go into Macbeth's castle.

> This neatly brings the comments about the first extract to a close.

On the other hand, we see a different side to Lady Macbeth's character in the second extract, where she is brutal and honest. She insults Macbeth for being weak by saying, 'When you durst do it, then you were a man', which shows that she knows how to manipulate people by taunting them.

In this extract Lady Macbeth's bloodthirsty character is shown through the vivid language she uses, such as 'dash'd the brains out', which immediately follows a moment when she had revealed some tenderness:

'I have given suck, and know
How tender 'tis to love the babe that milks me:'

> Extended comments here because this is the most revealing extract. Note the 'point, evidence, comment' technique. The point made in the introduction about Lady Macbeth's manipulative character is picked up and expanded.

This shows how she seems to have burnt out and rejected all her warm, human feelings.

We see that she taunts her husband when he has doubts about the enterprise. She mocks him, 'When you durst do it, then you were a man'.

However, the third extract, towards the end of the play, shows us that Lady Macbeth is not as strong as we thought. Here her actions, walking and talking in her sleep, show a very different side to her character. It shows she is troubled and seems to have developed a conscience. There is dramatic irony when the doctor says 'You see, her eyes are open', because unknown to him, his words tell the audience that Lady Macbeth can see events in the past more clearly. Finally her conscience troubles her. She tries to rid herself of the guilt she feels by symbolically rubbing her hands. 'Out damned spot', she cries as if she could wash away her guilt as easily as she washed away Duncan's blood on the night of the murder. Previously she had mocked her husband, 'Fie my lord, fie! A soldier and afeard?' Now it is she who realises that 'the old' man's blood has come back to haunt her.

> By commenting on the dramatic irony of the doctor's words, the student gains extra credit as it shows a high level of knowledge and understanding.

The three extracts each show a different side to Lady Macbeth's character: the charming but dishonest hostess, the manipulative and brutal wife and the guilt-ridden sleepwalker. In presenting these contrasts, Shakespeare has created an interesting character who holds the attention of the audience as her personality changes and develops throughout the play.

> The student brings the essay to a definite conclusion by making a general comment.

OVERALL COMMENT

This essay shows a high level of understanding and knowledge of the play, which includes an awareness of the audience. Points have been supported by appropriate quotations and interesting observations made. The essay structure relies on a straightforward examination of the extracts in chronological order, but is thorough and well organised. The spelling is accurate. The vocabulary and expression are impressive in places.

This answer would achieve a level 7 in the Test.

REVISION SESSION 2

(pages 66–67)

WRITING A RESPONSE TO TASK 2: HENRY V
(page 66)

TASK 2 Henry V
Act 1, Scene 2, lines 273–297

> **How does Shakespeare develop a mood of anger and tension in this extract to maintain the interest of his audience?**

If you have chosen to write your response using the chronological structure outlined in option 1 on page 67, you should have drawn your examples from those highlighted for you in the text extract, bringing out the increasing tension with which Henry addresses his audience. Make sure that you have at least one example to illustrate Shakespeare's use of language and imagery and show how it contributes to the anger and tension.

If you have chosen option 2, your response should be organised so that you have a paragraph discussing each of the devices outlined in the bullet points on page 67. The annotation of the text and the highlighting should have enabled you to select appropriate quotations.

Remember that these three points can be adapted and used to help you analyse any text, from any play, in order to respond to a question that concerns how Shakespeare creates or develops a mood. Look for:

1 The effect of the language (using Henry's speech as an example):
• choice of words – anything striking, unusual, e.g. 'dazzle', 'vengeance'
• the way they sound – words can be soft-sounding in a love scene, harsh in an argument (as 'mock' and 'strike' are in Henry's speech), brittle in a storm
• the links between them – what might the words have in common with one another, e.g. 'majesty', 'glory', 'king', 'throne', 'state', 'greatness'
• their associations with other things – what do they make you think of, e.g. 'well-hallow'd cause' – something that is hallow'd is holy, from God, making it sound as if God is on Henry's side.

2 Shakespeare's use of imagery and other devices such as alliteration
Shakespeare uses word-pictures (images created through figurative language such as metaphors, similes, personification) to help his audience see things that cannot be shown or to make them think about other things. For example, when Henry uses the metaphor 'my sail of greatness', we imagine the large sail of a ship, waving like a flag or a signal in the sea. Through this image, Shakespeare is hinting to his audience that Henry will actually set sail to conquer France.

3 The effect that the extract creates on others
This includes the characters in the play, as well as the audience.

Think to yourself:

  • How do the other characters respond to each other?
  • If someone was saying these words to me, how would I react?
  • How does Shakespeare want the audience to respond?
  • Does this extract interest the audience? Why? How?

REVISION SESSION 3

(pages 68–69)

WRITING A RESPONSE TO TASK 3: MACBETH
(page 68)

TASK 3 Macbeth
Act 5, Scene 1, lines 39–73

As the Doctor, write a personal and confidential account of what he has observed during his visit.

When asked to write as a character, check that in your response you have:

1 written in the first person throughout – as if you were the character;
2 focused clearly on the extract, drawing out points and using quotations;

3 kept in character – in this example, the Doctor would not write in an informal tone, making such comments as 'the queen is crackers';

4 committed no anachronisms: this means that everything you write needs to fit in with the time in which the play was set, so – no phone calls, driving cars etc.;

5 shown that you understand the play and the context of the extract.

Extract from a sample response:

5 – shows knowledge of the context

Three nights ago the Queen's serving maid mysteriously called me to Dunsinane, the King's castle, because she was anxious about her mistress and wanted my professional opinion concerning her condition. I went with some trepidation as I know there are rumours of an uprising and the King has a reputation for violent outbursts when he is crossed. Nevertheless, I could not neglect my duty to a patient. For two nights I observed nothing out of the ordinary, and was beginning to think this was a false mission. Tonight, however, by witnessing the Queen's strange and sinister behaviour, I may have placed my own life in danger.

1 – written in the first person

Whilst watching in the chamber with the gentlewoman, I saw the Queen emerge carrying a candle, her eyes were open but her senses were shut. Then I observed her rubbing her hands as if washing them, uttering the words, 'Yet here's a spot' and 'Out damned spot' as she did so. These words seemed harmless enough, but those that followed began to send a chill down my spine. The notes I made at the time help me now to recall her speech accurately:

2 – focused on the extract, using references and direct quotations

'' Tis time to do't. – Hell is murky!'

3 – in character, Doctor shows these feelings at the end of the scene

Do what, I wonder? Mention of hell suggests something evil. Then,

'Fie, my lord, fie! a soldier, and afeard?
What need we fear who knows it, when none can call our power to account?'

Here was a woman afraid of nothing, or so it seemed. Of course she is right, no one can question the actions of a King. But what had they done that could have been questioned? I am afraid the answer followed:

4 – in keeping with the times, Macbeth as king would have been all-powerful

'Yet who would have thought the old man to have had so much blood in him?'

'The old man', could she mean Duncan? Did they murder Duncan? Is this the horrific secret that causes her to walk at night with a troubled conscience?

REVISION SESSION 4

(pages 70–71)

WRITING A RESPONSE TO TASK 4: MUCH ADO ABOUT NOTHING

TASK 4 Much Ado About Nothing
Act IV Scene 1, lines 288–313
In this extract, from *Much Ado About Nothing*, Beatrice gives Benedick a challenge. You have been asked to direct this part of the scene to help the other students in your class gain a better understanding of the two characters and their situation.
Write an explanation to the two actors playing the parts of Beatrice and Benedick, outlining the effect you want to create and how it could be achieved.

In this task or any other similar question on a different extract or play, check that you have brought out the following points:

> **Never forget that the audience's needs are central to all of these points.**

Context and character

Have you considered:

✓ what has just happened before the extract?
✓ the motivation of the characters?
✓ their general behaviour to each other?
✓ what hidden messages their words might convey?

(With special reference to the given extract from Much Ado About Nothing)

- Beatrice loves Benedick, but doesn't want to make her feelings obvious – how have you addressed this point?
- She wants him to prove his love for her by asking him to do something that is brave and dangerous, but she doesn't really want him to be hurt – tricky! How have you shown that she is concerned but direct in her request?
- Benedick loves Beatrice, but doesn't want to do something too risky. How have you overcome this problem?
- Benedick and Beatrice love to play word games with one another, this is part of a sparring relationship they have with one another. How have you brought out the potential humour that lies beneath their words, even when dealing with a serious subject?

Delivery and expression

Have you commented on:

✓ The general tone that each character uses?
✓ Bringing out key words and ideas contained in the language?
✓ Examples of how you think characters should say a particular key line?
✓ Dramatic irony and its effect (this is when the audience is aware of something that the characters on stage are not aware of)?

Body language

Have you given some indication of how you would like the character to behave and move, such as:

✓ Facial features – especially the eyes?
✓ Hands and arms?
✓ Body movements?
✓ The way they sit or stand?

Action and effect

Have you written about:

✓ Where the characters are on the stage in relation to one another and what this tells us about them?
✓ Their movements as the scene progresses?
✓ How they move in response to one another?
✓ The audience's dramatic awareness?

Note

How much you can say about any of the above will largely depend on the extract you have been given and the time constraints of the test, but try to cover at least one point from each of the above.

Extract from sample answer discussing body language:

During this part of the scene, Beatrice would want to keep herself as far from Benedick as possible. This is to avoid any advances that he might make towards her. Until he has granted her request, she would hold herself in a tense and upright way, perhaps standing sideways to help her to avoid direct eye contact with Benedick. On the other hand, Benedick's body language would be more open and friendly – he wants Beatrice to love him, but he doesn't want to give in to her. Through his looks and glances he will be trying to make direct eye contact as he pleads with Beatrice. He will use his arms and hands a great deal when talking.

Glossary

adjective a word that describes something: 'the <u>tall</u> cupboard', 'the <u>round</u> balloon'

adverb a word or phrase that tells you more about a **verb**, an **adjective**, or even a whole **sentence**: 'Chris whistled <u>softly</u>', 'The <u>brightly</u> coloured rug', 'I will give it to you <u>tomorrow</u>'

advise to offer information and suggestions for how someone should act or behave in a particular situation

alliteration the effect created when words next to or close to each other begin with the same letter or sound: '<u>s</u>everal <u>s</u>ilent <u>s</u>lithering <u>s</u>nakes'

annotate to mark up with your own notes, which are usually made in the margin

argue to put forward a viewpoint

assonance the effect created by the repetition of vowel sounds: 'gr<u>ee</u>n f<u>ie</u>lds'

clause the building block of a **sentence**; each clause must contain a verb and normally includes a subject as well. Some sentences consist of a single clause: 'It was snowing.' Other sentences consist of two or more clauses: '<u>It was snowing</u> and <u>we were cold</u>.'

complex sentence a sentence containing one main **clause** and one or more subordinate clauses

compound sentence a sentence made up of two or more main clauses joined by a **conjunction** such as 'and' or 'but': 'Laura went skating but Judy stayed at home.'

conjunction a word that joins parts of sentences: 'and', 'but', 'if', 'although', 'as', 'where'

connective a word or phrase that links clauses or sentences. Connectives can indicate addition ('also', 'furthermore'), opposition ('however', 'on the other hand'), reinforcement ('besides', 'after all'), explanation ('for example', 'in other words'), lists ('first', 'finally'), result ('therefore') and time ('meanwhile', 'later').

director the person in charge of a production of a play or film. The director is concerned not only with how the words should be spoken and how the characters move and act, but

also with how the costumes, lighting and scenery contribute to the overall effect.

dramatic irony the effect created in a play when the audience knows what is really going on but one or more of the characters does not

entertain to keep someone or an audience interested or amused

fact a piece of information that is true; compare **opinion**

fiction literature, especially novels and stories, that describes imaginary events and people. Sometimes the setting may be a real place, or the story may be based on a real character or historical event.

figurative language the use of words or expressions in an abstract or imaginative way to create a particular impression or mood. Imagery such as **metaphors**, **similes** and **personification** are examples of figurative language.

first person a way of describing a text in which the writer or speaker refers to himself or herself by using the pronouns 'I' and 'we'; compare **second person**, **third person**

imagery the use of language to create a vivid image or picture; **metaphor**, **simile** and **personification** are forms of imagery

impersonal writing that uses the **third person** ('he', 'she', 'it', 'they')

inverted comma a punctuation mark used to show the beginning and end of direct speech ('Look out!' shouted Ali) or to highlight a particular word (the word 'genuine'). Also known as quotation marks.

irony a type of humour in which words are used to imply the opposite of what they normally mean

metaphor a form of **imagery** when one thing is said to be another: 'You are my sun and moon'

mnemonic a strategy or method of remembering something: 'There is <u>a rat</u> in separate'

narrative voice the 'person' that a writer uses to narrate a story: the two main narrative voices are **first person** (using 'I' and 'me') and **third person** (using 'he' and 'she')

non-fiction any form of text that is not **fiction**

noun a word that names an object or quality: 'dog', 'luck'

onomatopoeia the effect created by words which copy the sounds associated with their meaning: 'crack', 'hiss'

opinion a belief or view about something or someone; compare **fact**

paragraph a section of a piece of writing, used to organise the argument or help readers follow the storyline. A new paragraph should mark a new topic or a change of focus; in dialogue, paragraphs mark a change of speaker.

personification a form of **imagery** when an inanimate object is described in language that relates to animals or humans: 'The tree whispered'

persuade to try to convince a reader or listener to accept a point of view

prefix a group of letters that can be added to the beginning of a word to change its meaning or function: '<u>un</u>known', '<u>dis</u>arm'

punctuation a way of marking text with symbols (punctuation marks) to help readers' understanding. The most common punctuation marks are: apostrophe, bracket, colon, comma, dash, exclamation mark, full stop, hyphen, inverted comma (speech mark), question mark and semi-colon.

rhetorical question a question that doesn't require an answer, used for dramatic or persuasive effect

rhyme a pattern that occurs when words or the endings of words share the same sound, especially in verse

second person a way of describing a text in which the writer or speaker refers to the reader or audience by using the pronoun 'you'; compare **first person**, **third person**

sentence a group of words that make sense. Sentences usually have a subject and a verb, begin with a capital letter and end with a full stop (or exclamation mark or question mark).